A Book of Our Own

A Book of Our Own

Works by Rochester-Area Bookstore Employees

Edited by

James E. Walker Patrick Callan
Abram Johnson Marc McGee

Tinnitus Publishing Co.
Rochester, NY

A Book of Our Own: Works by Rochester-Area Bookstore Employees would have either not been possible or have been of lesser quality were it not for the generous assistance and support of the following people:
God, Our loving parents and families, Susan Lusignan, Richard LaPointe, Dan Berube, Colosseum Caffe, Dean Klingler, Marc Krolczyk, Kristine Matt, Gitsis, Caffeine, Jennifer Reall, Kevin Hamblin, The Bug Jar, Scott Erb, Dan Zicari and Judy Woodhams.

A Book of Our Own: Works by Rochester-Area Bookstore Employees

Library of Congress Catalog Card Number: 95-62007

First Edition Paperback
10 9 8 7 6 5 4 3 2 1
ISBN 096457117X

Cover Artwork "Biological Timeclock"
by Christie Becker

Cover Design by Kevin Hamblin

Hendrickson,R. (1990). *American Literary Anecdotes.*
New York: Facts on File, Inc..

Type and inside design by Kevin Hamblin:
KMH Visual Communications
PANTONE313@AOL.com

Tinnitus Logo
Original Design by:
Judy Woodhams
Finished Design by:
Kevin Hamblin

For Ordering Information Contact:
Tinnitus Publishing Co.
P.O. Box 93340
Rochester, NY 14692

for all bookstore employees

[William Faulkner] briefly worked in a New York bookstore in 1921. According to his employer: "He was an excellent book salesman, almost insulting customers who picked up what he considered worthless books, and pressing better books upon them with the words, 'Don't read that trash; read this.'"

-from *American Literary Anecdotes*

Contents

Introduction

For the artist working in a bookstore, being surrounded by so much published work can, at times, inspire great creativity. Other times, it can intimidate to the point of creative paralysis.

But we editors have worked in Rochester-area bookstores for the past few years and have had the pleasure of discovering and enjoying first-hand the artistic talent that bookstores seem to magnetically attract. At work, we discuss our various projects over bookshelves on the sales floor and over coffee in the back. We stuff our writing into each other's mailboxes and get honest, constructive feedback. After work, we attend each other's art shows and coffee house performances. And it's been through these experiences that something has become very clear: we're a diverse, active community of artists, and we're *good.*

It is this belief that inspired the establishment of Tinnitus Publishing Company and this, our first project, *A Book of Our Own,* over coffee and cheesecake at the Colosseum Caffe on Park Avenue almost a year ago.

Since then, we have twice visited the over fifty bookstores in the greater Rochester area soliciting submissions of works to be considered for this book. The volume of submissions was tremendous. This made our next task of selecting pieces for this book both very difficult and very pleasurable.

After months of discussing, debating, and sometimes arguing, we have chosen over thirty pieces that we are proud to call *A Book of Our Own: Works by Rochester-Area Bookstore Employees.* We hope that our readers will agree that this book represents well the diversity and talents of those in our chosen profession.

The Editors
October 1995

There's a world we live in as children

by Jessica Hill

There's a world we live in as children

that's forgotten. How nothing made sense,
but did. We've come back from those places
that no one's been traveling, swift as birds,
caught in spring rain. I was bird too,
wanting to believe it, but my arms didn't move like wings.

Once, I heard my own voice rise
echoing long rooms into existence.
But words are empty without listening, so I stayed
dreaming, lifting myself through trees,
waiting for something else to need my telling.

Now, after a storm has beat the low branches
against our house, I want to believe
in something else's telling, because even lightning
shapes celebration and makes us whole again.

Sometimes even waking into sunrise
is the only thing that makes us live.

First, I hardly noticed

by Jessica Hill

First, I hardly noticed

the Jeep rolling over, my slow
downward spiral of the world
or the earth turning, and having
landed wedged into hill and mud, still
waiting for the accident to begin.

At seven I stabbed my own
fist into my mother's sewing sheers,
not understanding the pure
sensation until the blood marked
the table in red sentences.

In our bed again, that hour before
we aren't alone anymore, my lips
trying to tell you things in two
places, between truth and my own
insecurities you're listening

with your eyes closing, your hand

around mine loosens, and all there is,
is the heavy pounding
of a heart or a basketball
two floors above.

The way we remember begins

by Jessica Hill

The way we remember begins

at five twenty-one, with a clear sky, driving
route 31 east, the truck in front swerving
into the left lane, a heavy stream of cars
coming and one's deserted in my lane.

Across the divider, shard glass sparkles
in a semicircle around a gray-haired woman
looking up from the shoulder of the road,
holding a man, holding his head.

A white car is stopped crooked
in the left lane, blood in thin streaks,
dark red painted on the driver's side door.
This time, her eyes closed.

Now it's my screen door on a black background,
letting the cat out, the door open again
and under the light there's a luna moth,
its wing ripped, and a woman

her hair mixed with sky, still holding
a man. But this time they're rocking
and his arms are at his sides. The cars still there,
two crooked, one in each lane.

Only the glass reflects moonlight. Maybe
I hear a cricket, maybe not,
but they're there rocking
and this time she doesn't look up.

Media Series: Manchurian Candidate
by Roy Sowers

Weaving

by Jayne Aquilina

CARRIE KNEW JAMES WAS HOME. WHEN the door slammed, the whole apartment shook. If she had been deaf, she still would have known it was 5:40, and he was home. Two thumps and his boots were off. A softer, shushing noise, and his jacket was on the floor. She pursed her lips. Sometimes he was like a little boy....

She took a breath to quiet her nerves and waited for him to enter the living room. She heard him stop in the kitchen to get a beer. She hoped there was some left, or she'd hear about it. She busied herself with rearranging her yarn and straw, drawing the mounds closer about her.

She was making a basket. Weaving one. She had just started it that day, since she realized that she was bored to tears with daytime television. She couldn't stand the game shows with all the flashing lights and screaming people, or the melodramatic soaps. She especially hated the commercials, constantly badgering her to buy laundry detergent for soft diapers and sugary breakfast cereals only a six-year-old could stomach. It had gotten to be too much for her, finally. She had to do something, call something into being. She shook off her throbbing headache and went out to the nearest craft store and bought thick, slick rope, a pile of narrow straw, and some skeins of different colored yarns. She had learned how to weave in school, and she knew she was good at it. She hadn't done it in years; she had never felt the need to. Now she hoped she could remember how it was done.

Now the basket was only a double fold of rope, wrapped and bound by straw for a few inches, then yarn. She was going to have a random pattern, nothing too complicated for her first try in years.

As she waited for James, she poked the needle with gray yarn between the new coil and the already-bound part of the rope, wrapping the woven white with color. She listened to James wash his hands at the kitchen sink and wondered if he would be angry with her for spending so much money on a new hobby. But he would understand — if he even thought of it. There was the chance he might not notice. Her husband entered the living room then, beer in hand, his red baseball cap with the Coca-Cola script logo on it tipped back on his head.

"Hi," she offered. "How was your day?"

He crossed to the window and looked out over the rooftops. "It's raining again." He set his beer bottle down rather heavily on the windowsill. Carrie watched the foam creep up inside the brown bottle, which tinted the foam a dull tan. He heaved a sigh. She watched striped-shirt shoulders rise quickly and fall just as fast. He seemed weary, and petulant.

Carrie felt she should go to him, but she didn't move. She focused on the craft in her hands. "How was work?" she asked, as she pushed the needle in again.

"Wet," he said, turning to her. His voice was a little lighter. The tension that had been growing in her neck loosened a bit. She pulled the needle out and up. "Wet," he repeated, "long, and boring."

"Did you have your truck fixed?"

"Yeah, on lunch. What's that?" He indicated the tangled mass of rope, straw, and yarn by pointing with the neck of the beer bottle.

"A basket." There was a skeptical pause. "Well, it will be. I'm weaving it."

James's voice was suddenly sarcastic. "Why?"

"I wanted to do something, James. I can't just sit around all day."

"Why not? I do."

"James— "

"I know, I know. 'Don't start.'" He took another swig of beer. "Dinner?"

"Leftovers?" she offered tentatively.

"Yeah, okay," he muttered, indifferent, and finished his beer.

Carrie started to rise, but decided to finish the length of yarn in her needle. James didn't seem to notice that she didn't get dinner right away. She wrapped the yarn around the rope with a steady rhythm — in, around, up, wrap. In again. James sat down, his eyes fixed on the flash of her needle in the dim half-light, and on the quiver of yarn as she pulled it taut. His hands gripped the arms of the chair, and when Carrie looked up at him she saw that his eyes had lost their focus. He wasn't staring at anything, now. In his sight, the needle was probably just an elongated blur in the shadows of the room.

She felt something invisible grip her heart. Carrie was held by the absence of life in James's eyes, and something close to terror welled up in her. Her hand with the needle kept moving, though the longer she kept weaving, the longer James would be mesmerized by the movement, and the longer that disturbing vacant look would stay in his eyes. James's head jerked, and he blinked.

Carrie rose from her nest of straw and yarn to make dinner. Once in the kitchen, she heard a click and then a murmur. James had turned on the evening news. The drone of the anchorman's voice soothed her somewhat as she began taking wrapped dishes out of the refrigerator. She noticed that there was one beer left. She opened it and brought it to James, touching the cold bottle to his shoulder to get his attention. He glanced up, surprised, but he smiled a little as he took the bottle from her.

The beer, she realized, was a new addition to their routine. Carrie returned to the kitchen thinking, when they had first gotten married (was it only three years ago?), they had loved the routine of their life together. They had welcomed it as a sign that their life was set forever. Pizza dinner on a Sunday night, garage sale shopping on sunny Saturdays...even the time schedule of the day — the fact that Carrie knew James would be home at 5:40 every night — let them know that they were a "married couple." The conventions of a newly-married couple were there: they had rented a little apartment "to start with," and James had gotten a job driving a delivery truck until he could find something more "in his field."

But they were still in the same apartment, and James hadn't been job hunting in over a year. Carrie wished she could help, but if James didn't send out résumés and track down the better jobs himself, all she could do was be patient. She was good at that. She supposed it was because she really didn't mind their life as it stood; she wasn't overly ambitious. It was James who often became depressed, and sulked.

She tried to bring up helpful suggestions every once in a while, gently, but James always took offense. Those times, often in the evening, took on their own pattern. They would argue, James would be louder, Carrie would cry, James would feel guilty and be silent. Then silence reigned for the rest of the night. The next day Carrie would be kind, and James would be penitent.

She knew he hated himself when he made her cry. He would go from a shout to a soft-spoken mumble, and he would try to stroke her shoulder to show he was sorry. She supposed he was extra careful with her since she had been sick. She had recovered, physically, months ago, but he still treated her as though she would break at the slightest upset. She had never planned to work; now, when they needed the money, he wouldn't even discuss the option. They didn't spend weekend days out anymore. And he was even afraid to make love to her. Somewhere deep inside, she knew, he was afraid she would get sick again. She knew it because she felt the same way, sometimes. Yet it went so far that they never spoke of it at all, couldn't even say the word "miscarriage." If they never said the word they would never have to think of it. At least, that seemed to be their unspoken agreement.

Carrie felt tears well up, her throat tighten. She nearly dropped the aluminum pie plate she was taking out of the oven, caught it, and placed it quickly on the stovetop. She took a deep breath, swallowed once or twice, and called James to come to the table.

"Just a minute," he called. From the lightness of the announcer's voice, Carrie knew that he was watching the sports report. She set the table and waited.

Eventually James turned off the set and sat down at the kitchen table. They ate in silence, quickly, as though they had more pressing matters they had to get to. Yet when they were finished, James went back into the living room and turned on the television again. Carrie scraped the remnants of reheated spaghetti into the garbage and put the dishes in the sink.

She left the dishes in the sink, unwashed. She stood in the doorway to the living room and watched James watch television. At his feet lay the tangled heap of materials that would be her basket. She could barely see the stuff in the dark living room. Afraid that James would hurt his eyes watching TV in the dark, she went over to the couch and flicked on the lamp. James squinted in the sudden bright glow flooding the room.

"What was that for?"

"It's dark!" she answered him, slightly incredulous.

James looked out the window as if he wanted to be sure. In the black square of glass was a burnished gold reflection of the living room — him sitting in his chair, Carrie behind him, wringing her hands as if she'd done something wrong, the multicolored flashes of the television screen, and something foreign on the floor — Carrie's basket. He looked from the window to her; she looked away and sat on the couch in the lamp's light. He returned his attention to the television. He didn't look at her again.

Carrie tried to watch the television as well, but she felt a headache begin to grow — the headache that came on exclusively in response to the chattering machine. She lunged for the partially-constructed basket. With hands shaking, though she didn't know why, she threaded her needle with a long cut of pink yarn and settled into the comforting monotony of her weaving. In, around, up, wrap. Her ragged breathing slowed, became even. After a while she became almost happy, watching her craft grow beneath her able fingers. In spite of herself, she began to hum a bit.

James heard and looked sideways at her. She didn't care. She kept humming and weaving. She finished the pink strand of yarn and cut a length of blue. When she finished that, she used some straw. She went faster and faster, with more rhythm, and James watched her. It couldn't be because he was interested — instead he looked compelled. He couldn't have ignored her now. She was creating something. This she could do, and do well. She could feel the power of her skill as a palpable tingling on her skin. Neither James nor any greater nature could take this away from her. And if this was hers, what would be next? She hummed her tune, her cheeks shining golden in the lamplight. Her hands and fingers were moving deftly, her needle glinting — a flash of fire.

James stared. Carrie was suddenly worried, and risked casting a quick glance at him. But his eyes weren't glazed this time; he was watching her intently. She kept weaving steadily. In front of him, the TV rattled on, ignored. Carrie wove. James watched, frozen. Slowly, a smile drew across her face.

It was wiped off quickly. James jumped up, turned the television off with a loud snap. "It's late," he said hollowly. "I'm going to bed." He waited for her to follow, like he always did. When James retired for the night, she always followed.

Tonight she remained where she was, needle poised.

James spoke again, and his voice was harsh. "It's late," he repeated. "Come to bed."

Carrie didn't move. She stared at her reflection in the window. There she was, sitting, her hand holding the needle, the beginnings of a basket in her lap, all lamplight and shadows. She looked for James, but he was blocked by the tall tabletop lamp beside her. The only thing the window reflected was the flood of golden light.

She felt a movement behind her. James brushed past her, stalked down the hall, and was gone. Carrie's hand moved, as if of itself, down toward the basket. She was weaving again.

Slowly her pace picked up again, the tune returned to her lips — softly, but steadily.

The apartment was silent, except for Carrie's humming. No sound came from James in the back of the apartment. She paused in her song and her weaving, and heard only the low buzz of the kitchen clock. The rain had stopped. The world outside was silent too. She reached down and cut another piece of yarn, this one yellow, and kept on weaving.

Poem of the Hungry Man

by Michael Tomczyszyn

My grey belly it gnawing
like the quiet
of an empty glove,
like my brain
when the sun go down —
painted yellow as little ones would —
or like my stone eyes.
That plum you hold
under cold faucet drip
it sure smell good...
so that splash of slivers
wetting the sleeve of your shirt
in dark weed slashes
it tickle my nose
and it make me think
that sweet bag of water
it belong good in my belly.

If I Did Not Know Better

by James E. Walker

He skied between countries:
France, Italy, Switzerland.
Stopping in broad daylight
for wine — hearty, red
warm laughter of easy friendships.
Quick goodbyes
then an embraced hike
and a wild ride —
aspen, birch, fir
to the cabin,
to his lover of few words
and her devoted eyes.
If I did not know better,
I would hate you, Hemingway.

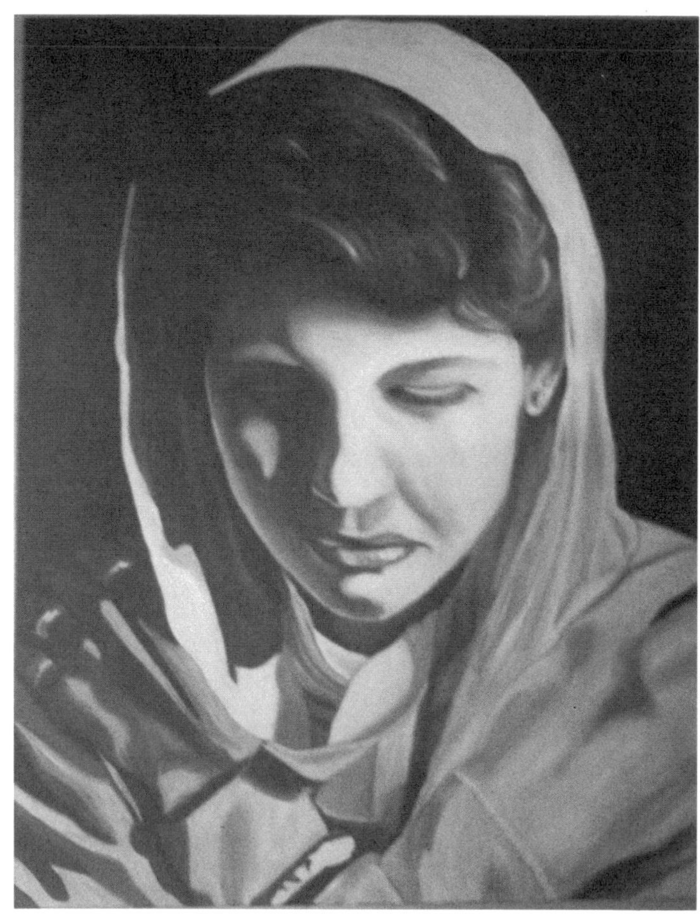

Mary by *Christie Becker*, oil on canvas, 32" x 40 1/2", 1989.

Dance Lessons

by Marc McGee

HER TRAILER'S WINDOWS WERE fogged because of the rain. Seth stood under a maple tree. Cool droplets of her sweat fell from the branches above and rushed down the back of his neck before they deltaed out. Cupping one hand, he lit a cigarette and stood puffing for a few minutes. Some nights he refrained from smoking. Tonight she couldn't see the headlights of a John Deere. Water gullied in his deep eye sockets, which he let pool. He wouldn't see anything tonight. No show.

He had first noticed her at Ray's moving-away party. She was gardening in worn tight jeans, red bandana, loose blouse sagging low enough to be painful. She at work in her matchbox yard while most of the rest of the park was enviously helping Ray celebrate. Ray had pulled Seth aside when he noticed the staring.

"Sometimes she sunbathes out back, naked. Nice rack, eh?" A giggle and an elbow to the ribs Ray used for emphasis. He growled and winked. Thelma overheard. She made Seth and the kids leave early. After she had a whiskey and the kids had gone to bed, she beat him with a broken broom handle. No man suffered bruises like that working in the thruway tollbooths, not unless they bent to get loose change and were blindsided, which had been known to happen.

Seth cursed out loud. He mashed the cigarette in the tree trunk and watched it, smoldering, drop. The windows weren't fogged at the top and he thought about climbing the tree. Against his better judgement, he jumped for the first branch, and wriggled his legs up and over. Sitting on the branch, he couldn't remember doing anything so straining since high school gym class.

Bits of wet bark clung to him like huge dandruff flakes. Of course, he'd have to think up an excuse during the night shift to explain to Thelma why he had become dirty. Not even the midnight manager cared how dirty Seth might be, his four fingers of scotch never making it below two before it was refilled. Seth had already used the excuse of falling from the fence, which he had to traverse, on his walk to work. That was the night she was pulling and twisting at her olive nipples in front of the mirror, and he came in his Dickies before he could even pull it out. She pulled at the nipples, pushed her robust bosom together, and twisted from one side to the other catching a profile in the mirror, poking and irritating them. He was frozen, hunched like an old man. His breathing became quicker than it had ever been. And before he knew what was happening the seizures hit like a tsunami. He had never experienced anything close to that with Thelma. Not even in the beginning when everything was near perfect. It seemed a demon was born along with their first child.

He had rolled in a patch of mud to disguise the smell and stain. When he stopped back home, she cussed him out for being so clumsy and for being late for work. She pulled matted locks of brown from the corner of her mouth, "I should shoot you like they do the horses at the track. You're not even good for glue. Now get to work before you get your sorry ass fired." That night at work, he had gotten so caught up in trying to recapture the feeling, he waved several cars into the coffee night without taking toll.

From the branch he was on he could still not see clearly into the bedroom. There was a faint image like a small mouth darting the bottom of a stream. He could tell which room she was in. He could also tell it was one of her active nights. She was a flurry of translucence.

She didn't have a routine schedule but she certainly did do many of the same exercises, all of them in the nude. Sometimes she danced with the lights on, and on bad nights with the lights off. Sometimes she sat motionless on the top of her bed, meditating. Sometimes she exercised, falling periodically to the floor, which forced him to get in dangerously close to the window or climb a tree to see. One night she pulled at her nipples.

He only had fifteen minutes to get to work. Ten minutes to get off, and five minutes to cross the trailer park, doubling back, cautiously, past his own trailer, jump the fence, and cross the field to the tollbooths. Seth stood on the branch to judge the view. He could only see her blonde hair tied in a bun. This kept it out of her face while she expended all the energy in her atomic young body. She was really moving tonight. He reached up for the next branch. He couldn't bear the thought of not getting off before work. It was the one thing he felt he deserved in life, the one thing his wife could not ruin.

The patter on the tin roof replaced the music which could sometimes be heard and seen shaking the baseboard and windows. The branch he was holding cracked. He caught himself but his head hit trunk. It was the same sound and pain he remembered from the fight with Thelma in the morning. Crack, thud. First she smacked the counter, and then she hit his skull. Crack, thud.

"Whaddya mean you're goin' to the track with Ray this weekend? There's no way in hell you're gonna throw away our money...my babies' money, drinking and gambling all goddam day with that no-good son-of-a-bitch.... What're you thinking? Don't you see you have a family to provide for? You have responsibilities.... Don't you ever consider us, you bastard? You're gonna bring that paycheck home to me tomorrow. Got it?" Crack, thud.

"Yeah." He rubbed his head and reached again. A determined pull and he was sitting one branch higher, looking at the commotion within.

From his crow's nest, Seth thought he saw two bodies moving as if they were promenading or, what he'd seen on the Lawrence Welk reruns, waltzing. Thelma always seemed to lose herself in the costumes and set drops of the show. It was one of the few occasions he felt like he had a real family. When he offered to take waltzing lessons at the fire hall with her, she spit her beer, guffawed, and shouted, "With your two left feet? Not a chance. I need a *Ginger* Rogers not a *Mister* Rogers."

He held the grapefruit back of his skull and tried to refocus. The wind picked up, blowing the rain sideways in convulsions. As far as he knew she'd never had anyone over to visit, besides her brother who was a stable boy. Ray had gotten a hot tip from the brother once when he was watching the trailer for his sister. Seth and Ray both lost a bundle. The brother apologized saying, "I hocked my sister's jewelry." They left him alone.

It would be strange for brother and sister to be dancing. That's what he was taught. The bodies passed to and fro with jerks and pauses of an evenly-matched tug-of-war. Skin flashed silver in the dim light. Long brown hair shown and bare ass. Definitely a man had entered her life. He found himself limp in his hand, rain rolling and dampening his underside. A quick, unbalanced flourish and the light went out inside. "Damn it." He pulled at it but the rain and this man provided nothing. He thought of her olive nipples being plucked and pushed by him. Nothing. Folding and zippering, he jumped from the second limb, jammed his knees and rolled over onto his back. He tucked the red bandana back into his pocket, resigned to defeat.

Staving off the waves of pain in his knees and head, Seth made his way around the side of the trailer closest to Ray's old home. Behind a small evergreen he peeked around and found no car in the short gravelled driveway. No car in the street, either. He wiped the water from his eyelids. "It's that goddam Ray. Fucker." He hadn't forgiven Ray the time he stole the young groomer from him after a day of sunburn and fourth places. He imagined Ray's rusted truck parked in the gravelled lot of Stoney's, his stuttering gait across the interstate.

Seth approached the porch, peering the neighborhood. The rotted wood moaned. The front door was open, just the screen was keeping him out. Pulling out his starchy hanky, he unscrewed the front porch light.

Whatever commotion caused the lamp to go out hadn't ceased. There was still movement. He had seen such whirling dervishes on public television and couldn't understand these fits. Thelma had laughed and whooped as she brought the Swansons into the room. The raunch of gravy stuck to his lungs as Thelma wailed right along with the television.

The rain patter waned and polka music waxed. Human sounds emanated but he could not distinguish whether they were pleasured or tortured. The sounds flowed through the screen like smoke through his filterless generic cigarettes. He drew it all in.

There was a woman's scream rivaling those of a surprised game show contestant. A loud clang followed. He pressed his nose to the screen door.

"Get off of me," the woman's voice cracked. It wasn't panicked. The second time was. "Please, get off!" There was a long silence and the laughter of schoolgirls.

She was being forced, he thought. He was torn. If it was Ray, would he let him join in? Ray owed him. There was also the time before they were married that Seth let Ray have his turn with Thelma. He owes me, he thought.

If it wasn't Ray, he'd have to stop the bastard, be the hero, and get it from her later. She'd have to if I saved her life, he thought. He'd probably be on the local news. That Gail Davis is real cute for an anchor woman. After the interview, she'd probably be so impressed he could have her, too.

Seth reached for the screen door handle. He hoped Ray was inside. A howl stopped him. It was a familiar howl, but unnameable. It floated just under his consciousness level. It was as distinct as a drunken conversation. He backed away. How would he explain to Thelma why he'd been in the right place at the right time to save this woman? She wouldn't believe him. The news would be bad. He would be a broken hero, Superman coming home to be beaten by Lois Lane. He couldn't help this woman if he wanted to.

He could hear it. "What the hell are you doing over at the hippie's trailer? Huh, Seth, huh? Is it free love, Seth? Free love. There's no such thing. Do you pay her, Seth? Is she your whore? You saved your little hippie slut from another scumbag?" Crack, thud.

He stepped backwards down the steps. He heard himself calling "Ray" under his breath. "Ray...Ray...." It was the sound of a wife's voice waking her husband as if a prowler were downstairs. He kept stepping backwards.

He was no hero. He had to be to work in two minutes. Turning around, he broke into stride, dodging muddy holes in the road.

Seth passed his trailer. The screen door was open and just

the T.V. lights flashed from the windows. When he came home in the morning he often found Thelma asleep in the chair, still in her clothes, *Good Morning America* preaching new recipes. She would send the kids off to school and then climb into bed with him and sleep the rest of the day. He didn't understand how anyone could sleep so much.

Seth brushed at his work clothes. "A car sprayed a puddle," he convinced himself. He saw his windows turn a foggy purple, then black. He looked back to make sure she hadn't seen him. He'd bring home that paycheck. She'd cash it or deposit it or do whatever she did with it. He'd ask Thelma again if she'd take dancing lessons with him. Seth could hear her laughter as he was jumping the last obstacle between him and his work.

from The Love Journal

By Todd Beers

1/12/95

10:30 p.m.

the new guy at work will jump at the chance to help somebody out. it doesn't matter who it is, and that's the beauty of it. he's environmentally conscious and put his wife through vet school by driving a blood mobile. one morning he helped a stranger move three counties over. in the afternoon he hauled 10 cords of wood for his seventh cousin, and that night made love to his wife like a husband possessed. he had a smile on his face all day long. i nicknamed him narc martyr because i'm suspicious.

1/14/95

3 a.m.

with a one-year-old son i have developed strange sleeping patterns. rem has become more frequent. last night i fell asleep on the kitchen floor and my eyes began to dart back and forth like two little black moons gone awry. this time i get arrested for cutting wood with my seventh cousin on state hunting ground. the younger man tells us how important rotting wood is to wildlife. i insist to the older man, the one who doesn't like music, that i am wildlife. two little black moons dart back and forth in the sky. three of us smile. the other one is confused. as my seventh cousin says, *native americans take only what they need and leave the rest*. a logger drives by for the second time and nods to the one who wasn't smiling. i flip the logger and his cellular phone off. i don't let the old man see me do this, because i don't want him to know that i know.

later, my cousin bill and i break from splitting wood and play a quick game of poker in a gentle snow storm. my cousin sees my cards, but like any good player with honor, he doesn't let on. our fingers are cold, and in this we are proud of the wood we gathered. a pregnant woman i am fond of walks to the mailbox with child in her arms. we need her to see the wood we have gathered. we want her to say, *wow, you guys got a lot of wood.* we would be proud like cave men. we make her say it. she knows this, and then she says it. she likes saying it though. bill asks her if she would put on a pot of coffee. when we go inside she's warm, the baby's warm and the coffee's warm.

1/18/95

11:30 p.m.

tuesday afternoon

twelve-year-old daughter bums
quarters from old-time alcoholics.
crusty, old bartender gives her a coke,
turns up the tijuana brass.
does a little flamingo twirl
with clenched fist, bends down
when no one is looking and says,
kissy. kissy.

1/30/95

11:50 p.m.

albany

little boy
with frock
buttoned
at the collar
bends in
the blue
wind
so he won't
lose
his acorn.
seven raisins
line his left
front pocket.
his name
in the afternoon.
a mother's voice.

Descent
by Gabe Billings

An Imitation of Life

By William Lung

THERE WERE TWENTY-SEVEN MILES between New Hope and Billings, or so the road sign said; twenty-seven miles which lay flat beneath the sun and the stars. The approaching warmer months would chase the snow into the ground and the air, leaving behind the bones of animals who could not escape their wintry graves. Soon after, the dust of the road and the surrounding terrain would be lifted off the blazing Montana floor by passing trucks and far-off mountain winds. On this section of I-54, through the rear- and sideview mirrors you could see the low buildings and farmhouses of New Hope disappear into the flatness. Mattie had seen this dissolution of New Hope as often as she had seen the resurrection of Billings. Driving towards Billings, the city would rise hazily from the plains, an oasis of seven-story buildings, warehouses and shops that made any memory of New Hope a forgotten one.

Mattie made this trip often enough to familiarize herself with the roadside skeletons which had lain still for years. She had begun to name them, in honor of old steadies who left her feeling used and unwanted. Mattie christened her first skeleton Junior, after her first boyfriend John Michael Young II. Junior had asked her to the Warner Township High School Spring

Cotillion of 1947. She almost fainted when he uttered the words, "Would you like to go to the Spring Cotillion with me?" It was then, during her first year at Warner High, that Mattie first felt the warmth of her blood rushing to the top layer of her skin, filling her with both shame and pride.

The preceding summer had brought record heat to the area and everything wilted under the sweltering sun, except Mattie. She withstood the sun as long as she could, and the prolonged heat softened her and made her bubble and burst out of her small linen blouses and sleight, pleated skirts. When the Warner boys began to notice her, Mattie began to feel the weight of their eyes press upon her bosom and buttocks. She would feel burdened beneath the weight, so her legs would give out and she'd stumble into the doors and walls and other stationary things at Warner High.

Soon after, the burdensome weight followed Mattie home, from bathroom mirrors to the glassy pond behind the barn. Mattie was thus rendered unable to negotiate the treacherous landscape of her father's ranch, which included: the two posts supporting the main house's awning, the wire fencing penning-up the chickens (which left a two-inch scar on the back of her right thigh), and the patches of grass upon which the cows would graze. Mrs. Doyle was concerned for her daughter but felt as helpless as Mattie in her newly-acquired awkwardness.

Ranching in Montana required low centers of gravity from its women so they could milk the cows, pitch the hay and bed down more easily with their husbands. With the help of the hearty foods culled from the ranch, mixed with the starch from Mrs. Doyle's ancestral Irish blood, Mrs. Doyle was brought closer to the Montana soil she worked so hard to manage. She carried herself gracelessly amongst the livestock, treading on the same dirt as the other brethren of the ranch. So when Mattie had her encounter with the wire fencing and her blood muddied the dirt she lay in, the most useful counsel Mrs. Doyle could give was, "Mattie, you just gotta be more careful!" No sage words concerning poise were offered because Mrs. Doyle had none.

Mr. Doyle would have been more helpful in regards to Mattie's poise and appearance, after all it was his genes showing prominence in her features: the thick auburn hair, the bright brown eyes, the body's defiance of gravity. Mattie's father moved around his ranch with great certainty. He could only watch his daughter and think what a fine job he and Mrs. Doyle had done. It was Mr. Doyle's genes which showed prominence in Mike, Chuck and Joey Doyle too, Mattie's brothers, and they had turned into fine specimens. Mr. Doyle didn't see Mattie's stumblings as anything peculiar, just a kid getting used to its new legs. He anticipated her growing into a fine young woman.

The Adams County Cattle Auction brought the Doyles into Billings in the fall of 1946. The prospects of selling his stock were particularly high and put Mr. Doyle in a generous disposition. With his wife and two oldest sons helping at the auction, Mr. Doyle sent his two youngest children off with a dollar each to spend in a soda shoppe, movie theatre, or however they chose. Joey was fifteen, a year older than Mattie, so Mr. Doyle felt comfortable enough to allow them to roam the streets of Billings. The Doyle children debated as to what it was they wanted to do most and settled upon taking in a movie at the Big Sky Orpheum, whose slogan was, "Where dreams come true!"

Though the marquee lights were not turned on during these daylight hours, the glare of the late morning sun on the big black letters, "*The Postman Always Rings Twice,* starring John Garfield and Lana Turner" made Mattie's eyes grow wider. Anticipation of the cool, dark air, the worldly newsreels and the roar of the MGM Lion made Mattie's heart beat more quickly; but her subsequent thoughts almost made her heart stop beating altogether. It was a John Garfield movie, a grown-up movie — they wouldn't be able to see it, and Joey had realized it too. Refusing defeat, Joey and Mattie walked around the corner into the back alley, where Mattie fell over pebbles and paper, not helped by the danger and excitement. The rear door was unlocked and unmanned; Joey made his way inside stealthily and Mattie did the best she could.

From within the dark theatre, the silhouettes of Mattie and Joey appeared against the glaring light from outside. The pair had passable adult figures: Joey carried his gravity-defying self with the same certainty as his father and Mattie's body made dark waves in the illuminated doorway. They seated themselves near the door and watched John Garfield enter through Lana Turner's kitchen door and press her up against the icebox.

Mattie watched Lana being held by John and the icebox, noting how she did not falter between the crushing weights. Lana did not succumb. She pressed back with her lips and with her arms embraced him tightly, pressing him even closer. Mattie's first instinct was to look away, cover her eyes, do anything not to see — but she couldn't help herself.

Mattie watched as Lana met every curve and line of John's body; the tight bodice and wide skirt of her dress allowed no light or air to pass between them. Mattie was amazed at how the dress kept Lana's softness firm and contained, how she didn't spill over and fall. Mattie looked down at herself. Her bosom pointed downward because its new weight made her hunch over. She saw her legs rest unattractively apart because there was too much weight for her to cross them. Mattie let out an exasperated breath and pushed away at the flesh on her thighs, hoping she could make it disappear. Disappointed at the refusal of her flesh to comply, she sighed and gazed up again at the screen.

Lana peeled herself off John and paced the room, walking to the stove, backing up against the sink and then the table. John shadowed her, walking to the stove, the sink, leaning against her against the table. They were engaged in a dance around the kitchen, where Lana led and John followed. He moved to hold her, kiss her, but her body refused by turning from him. Lana's legs took steps away from John, uncertain that away was the direction they wanted to go. Lana returned to the icebox, her back pressed against it; she breathed deeply and her bodice rose higher and higher and stayed there, till she exhaled. She stood, her legs beneath her, and this time John stayed back and did not follow.

Mattie breathed with excitement and anxiety as Lana had, and her back pressed up against the seat. She was surprised to feel herself grow taller. Mattie's head turned to Joey, then cautiously to her other side to see that no one else had noticed her. She was anxious to stand and test her own legs, to see if she could defend herself against the seats and the floor. But Mattie contained herself and sat through the remainder of the movie with her legs resting apart, absently shaking.

"The End" appeared on the screen and Mattie quickly rose to her feet, her knees promptly buckling beneath her. She closed her eyes tightly and breathed in the smell of the popcorn which she now laid next to on the floor. Joey offered a hand but Mattie refused, determined to stand on her own. Using the seats as crutches, Mattie clambered to her feet, rolled her eyes and followed Joey out the back door.

When the Doyles returned home, Mattie ran to her room and faced her standing mirror. She breathed and watched her bosom rise and herself grow. Mattie had lifted herself up, redistributed her weight. She turned to see if the improvement applied also to her backside, and it did. She attempted to walk from side to side, watching her legs carry her body without faltering too much. Mattie stared at herself in the mirror till dinner and liked what she saw.

For several months afterward, the image of Lana Turner remained in Mattie's mind. From the hayloft, Mr. Doyle would watch Mattie ride Sudie, her chestnut filly. She would mount Sudie and sit up, rather than fall forward and lose her face in the horse's auburn mane. From the kitchen window, Mrs. Doyle would see Mattie walk amongst the chickens as she fed them, heaving her chest to attain equilibrium. Mattie looked like the rooster that occupied the roost, except she fell off her perch from time to time, but these times came fewer and farther between. The two posts, the wire fencing, and the grass were no longer adversaries in Mattie's struggle to walk.

When she awoke in the morning and went to bed at night, or had any opportunity in between, Mattie would look at herself in the mirror. She would correct herself whenever her bosom pointed towards the floor, dragging her shoulders and head along. Mattie would then remember to inhale and once again she would rise to a height of 5'5 3/4". At school, the girls' bathroom became Mattie's most frequented place outside of class. There too, she'd survey her appearance and would not leave until she was satisfied. The other girls stood and were witness to Mattie defying gravity. They would remark what a change she had undergone; was it new clothes, a new coiffure? She would not answer the girls affirmatively, leaving them mystified.

It was upon leaving the girls' bathroom on one of these occasions, that Mattie's bosom was confronted by the torso of John Michael Young II, Junior. He excused himself for his clumsiness and she lowered her head in embarrassment. The ensuing conversation included a formal introduction because although they attended the same school, they'd never come in contact with one another. Even if Junior had met her before, he wouldn't have recognized the old Mattie from the one who stood before him now. The tops of her blouses could now be seen since she stopped hunching. Light which had once been obscured by her drooping now fell on her attire. Her skirts would stand and sway instead of mopping the floors of Warner High. Junior thought her a sight to behold, and after seventeen minutes of conversation, he uttered his memorable words.

After the Senior Prom, the Spring Cotillion was the second most anxiously-awaited event at Warner Township High School. New dresses were bought and sewn, suits cleaned and pressed. In this field, Mrs. Doyle was more than qualified to offer some assistance. Having made dresses all her life, Mrs. Doyle was able to pattern a full-length dress of pink taffeta with white satin trim. In the dress, Mattie curved on top, and the rest of her was lost in the wide skirt.

The gymnasium was filled with teenagers dancing to the croonings of Rudy Vallee. On Junior's arm, Mattie looked like a giant corsage, at home amongst the cotillion's decorative theme of flowers. She was too shy to look at Junior and too nervous not to wonder what her feet would do. While they first danced, Junior held her at a comfortable arm's length. Mattie looked down at her feet, trying to keep track of where they were, but all she saw was pink taffeta.

She remained staring at pink taffeta while he attempted to converse with her, while they drank punch against the wall, while they danced the next two dances. During that third dance, Junior held her a little closer. He could feel the swoosh of pink taffeta on his pant legs. Mattie moved closer without any voiced opposition. During the fourth dance, Junior pulled her closer still, and Mattie shuffled her feet to prevent herself from falling forward into his arms.

During the fifth dance, Junior pulled her closer still so their torsos would touch every time Mattie breathed. She tried to keep her pink taffeta from being crushed against Junior's body. She tried to keep their bodies from being too close, so she breathed less fully, taking smaller, faster breaths. But Mattie's short, quick breaths made her head dizzy, and the lack of air made her bosom tilt forward. Beneath the hot, gymnasium lights and the garlands of spring blossoms which adorned the rafters, Mattie stumbled and fell.

Everyone watched Mattie recover quickly, and Junior asked if she was OK. Mattie said yes and they promenaded to the punch bowl and she declined any further offers to dance. Since this was the only blemish on the evening, Junior extended Mattie an invitation to the New Hope Ice Cream Parlour for the following weekend.

At the ice cream parlour, Junior and Mattie sat themselves on stools at the counter. This time, Mattie felt relieved to be sitting on anything that would give her support, other than the floor. Mattie ordered for herself a cherry ice cream sundae, while Junior had a banana split. Sitting at the counter, Mattie did not have to face Junior directly; she could answer his questions with a slight tilt of her head and he would hear her. Mattie did not offer any questions of her own. All she did was answer his, which left Junior feeling uneasy.

So continued the remainder of their second date, and their third date and their fourth date. It was not for lack of trying on Junior's part; Mattie just hadn't mastered the fine techniques of talking to boys who were not her brothers. Junior was thus prompted to utter the words that remained even more memorable in Mattie's head: "Mattie, I don't think we should go steady anymore." For although Mattie had a fine body, she was still a nobody.

For the next two years, Mattie was propositioned by various boys at Warner High to go to movies, picnics, dances, but she declined them all. The words of John Michael Young II rung in her head. Mattie would still stand in front of mirrors, staring hard at her rounded bosom and hips, at her legs which stood firm and never failed her again after the Spring Cotillion. Mattie even mastered pivot turns in front of the mirror so she could survey her front, back and the radiating flair of her skirts. But in the mirror, she still could not see what Junior had not seen in her.

During these two years, Mattie thought often of Lana and wondered why John had wanted her so much. She would hear reports of Lana on the radio news programs and read about

Lana in the gossip columns of the local paper.

"Did you hear Lana Turner was sitting in some drugstore in Hollywood and some movie producer saw her and signed her up right there?"

"I sure did. Sitting in a drugstore minding her own business and just like that, she's a movie star. Can you imagine?"

"It's fate, I tell you. A girl as beautiful as that was just meant to be a movie star."

"I hear she's making another movie with Clark Gable!"

"No!"

"Yes!"

"Can you imagine?"

People would regard any information they had or knew about Lana as bringing them closer to being important, or at least bringing them closer to Lana. Everyone talked about Lana as if she were their daughter, sister, niece or neighbor, but never, never was she talked about as if she were a mother. Mothers didn't look the way Lana looked. What Mattie could gather about Lana was that she was discovered at Schwab's Pharmacy in Hollywood by a big movie producer, and that her first part was as an extra in *A Star Is Born* in 1937. Mattie read the paper daily, listened to the radio reports and to all the talk of townsfolks, and thought to herself, "Why can't *I* be Lana Turner?"

In the fall of 1948, Mattie again accompanied her father to Billings for a cattle auction, without Joey. She'd been to Billings numerous times over the years for Christmas shopping, school clothes, and movies. Mattie had seen many movies at the Big Sky

Orpheum, "Where dreams come true!", but the movies she could see did not star the likes of Lana Turner or John Garfield. On the ride to Billings, Mattie's thoughts returned to the image of Lana pressed between John and the icebox. She wanted so much to see the image again, to understand why John wanted Lana.

Mattie knew she'd be allowed to shop and browse the streets of Billings by herself. She also knew that *Homecoming* was showing at the Big Sky Orpheum, starring Lana Turner and Clark Gable. But her thoughts and devising were interrupted on I-54 by the pickup's flat front tire. Mattie exited the cab as Mr. Doyle began repairs; she wandered around the truck, and then some yards down the interstate.

Sun-bleached bones were the only remains of a wolf, lying a few feet from Mattie. She had seen dozens of skeletal types growing up on the ranch, and this was one she was familiar with: the elongated face and jaw, the thin, sleek body frame. Mattie approached the bones. She replayed the image of Lana and John and the icebox while the words, "Mattie, I don't think we should go steady anymore" echoed in her mind. Her full, firm steps pounded the dust off the road as she grew closer. She saw the picture and heard the words: Lana, "Mattie...", John, "I don't think we should...", the icebox, "go steady anymore." The image and the words alternated in her head, competing for her attention.

Mattie walked right up to that skeleton and stared hard at the emptiness which resided between its bones. She raised her foot to kick in the skull, and dirt flew with bone fragments through the air. It landed under a cover of dust — a scattered pile of bones, the skull upside down. The dispersed remains marked the most distinguishing feature of Mattie's first skeleton, for she would never be so intimate again with fleshless matter. As Mattie turned back towards the truck she allowed the words, "Damn you, Junior!", to escape her clenched teeth. As the pickup resumed its journey to Billings, Mattie watched as Junior and New Hope receded into the distance.

Alone in Billings, Mattie made her way to the Big Sky Orpheum. She stopped in front of a store window, looking at her reflection imposed upon the words, "Toler's Discount Hardware." Mattie moved slowly, turning from one side to the other, pretending to look at various makes of hammers. She saw her bosom fill her cream blouse and grey sweater impressively. She saw women and teenage girls lacking in stature pass behind her, and became confident in her adult form.

Mattie's legs supported her handily as she waited on line to purchase her ticket. No doubtful looks or questioning tones were directed at her. Proud of her deceit, Mattie seated herself in the very last row, up against the wall. She watched, as "Clark Gable and Lana Turner in *The Homecoming* " appeared on the screen, while the music swelled with high-pitched violins. Mattie's legs shook anxiously as she fixed her eyes on the screen. This is what she had been waiting for.

Mattie watched as Lana strode towards the fireplace, bent over and stoked the fire. Clark stood in the scope of her warmth.

Lana returned to the table and retrieved her cigarettes. She reached for her case and offered one to Clark, and lit him up. Lana and Clark seated themselves on the sofa and conversed about sad, regretful things. When she inhaled, she pursed her dense lips, enveloping the tip of the cigarette. She took two breaths: one short one, then a longer, slower one. Exhaling, Lana tilted her head slightly back while lingering bands of smoke ascended in ribbons around her head. She looked at Clark when he spoke, her eyes piercing the smoke, her cigarette poised between her fingers. Lana then looked down, avoiding the white bands, the heat of Clark's gaze, the melancholy of her own words.

Mattie watched as the import of their words fell down like rain from the cloud of smoke which served as the ceiling of their dismay. She wanted to see if her sadness would fall out and lie there too, mute and heavy. Mattie watched Lana rise from the sofa and return to the fireplace. Lana's eyes surveyed the silence of the room and then rested on Clark, telling him what he had been denying. Mattie's eyes stared at Lana's and stared at Clark's, wanting to tell them of her own dismay.

On the ride home to New Hope, Mattie was preoccupied with smoke and sadness as she stared at the oasis of Billings disappearing in the dust and haze. At home, Mattie went into her parents' room and snuck one cigarette out of an open pack lying on the night table. Then she went into the den and snuck one from the pack resting on top of the radio. She waited till

Mr. Doyle undressed at dusk to shower, then snuck one from the pack in his jeans pocket. Mattie stole the cigarettes in small increments so no one would notice. She repeated this routine, sneaking in and out of rooms till she had an ample supply.

One Saturday morning, earlier than usual, Mattie awoke. Grabbing a handful of the pilfered cigarettes, a book of matches and one of Mr. Doyle's heavier jackets, Mattie went out behind the barn. She placed a cigarette between her lips and put a flame up to the tip, but it didn't light. She tried another match and again she failed. Then her memory returned to Lana, and it occurred to her to take two breaths while she lit the cigarette — a short one, then a longer one.

She stared at the smoldering orange ember, burning two inches from her face while she began to drown in the pool of smoke that occupied her chest cavity and mouth. Mattie dropped the cigarette and exhaled a river of white smoke. The determined girl tried again after regaining her composure, and again and again. It required several Saturday mornings before Mattie felt she had mastered the technique and acquired the taste. Mattie was satisfied when she could finally inhale, pause, then exhale and watch the blue creases of Montana sky emerge from the billowing white smoke.

At Warner High, Mattie would still frequent the restroom, but now, along with surveying her appearance, she smoked too. She would join the older girls as they opened the windows and exhaled white puffs which would rise and get lost amongst the clouds. Now Mattie was more than just a body. People would remark on her appearance, but then voice their surprise concerning her new activity.

"Did you hear about Mattie Doyle? She smokes."

"No!"

"Yes!"

"I never would've guessed."

Students at Warner High forgot about Mattie's swerving body for a time, and once her lips remained permanently pursed from smoking, they regarded her as someone new. One of Mattie's smoking acquaintances arranged a blind date for her with a boy who had heard about the new-and-improved Mattie. The boy was Tommy Mullins.

Tommy became the second skeleton that Mattie christened on that section of I-54. Tommy lay about one hundred yards further down from Junior on the interstate. He had probably been a bull or horse of some kind; Mattie couldn't tell because she was never close enough to inspect. Tommy was inducted into the peculiar halls of Mattie's mind, as she continued to map out a trail of romantic roadkill.

For their first date, Tommy Mullins took Mattie to the rodeo. There, amongst the bulls, horses and rodeo clowns, Mattie felt much at home. Mattie and Tommy watched the cowboys rope the steer and the trick riders stand on and bounce off the galloping horses. Tommy offered Mattie a smoke and she accepted. They conversed amidst the rising smoke and the sounds of clapping hooves and raucous applause. Mattie forgot about the rodeo as she stared into Tommy's face while he spoke, his hay-colored hair slicked back, smoke creeping from his nostrils. She listened to him speak and responded with short affirmations, lengthy digression and statements all her own. Mattie could feel the lightness of her own words rise with the smoke from her mouth.

Mattie and Tommy became the talk of Warner High; going steady with Tommy Mullins had elevated Mattie to a higher status. They could be seen holding hands on the front walk of the premises in the morning and smoking along the back roads on their way home. But Tommy soon tired of Mattie, and she heard he was interested in another girl through the same talk that had been circulating about the two of them. After Junior and Tommy came Pete, Ronald, Jim and Lucky. The section of I-54 between New Hope and Billings was littered with the debris of Mattie's heart.

By graduation, Mattie had tamed and conquered her body. She could make it do whatever she wished, so she dragged it to Billings to find a job. She became the head salesclerk at Noble's Five-and-Dime. Through the store window, her place behind the register was visible from the street and invited passersby to come and look. She still lived at home with her parents and drove Mr. Doyle's old pickup back and forth between New Hope and Billings. After work sometimes, Mattie would go to the Big Sky Orpheum and see the latest movie starring Lana, but she didn't have to sneak in anymore. She would watch Lana as different incarnations, but what first attracted her was always there: the same walk, same breathing, same pursed lips, same sadness. Mattie would disregard Lana's leading men and just stare at Lana, who filled the screen and the emptiness of Mattie's eyes.

Feeling anxious and the void burning within her, Mattie decided to enter the Miss Adams County Beauty Pageant. She prepared herself well, traversing the confines of her room in a bathing suit and heels, talking to her reflection in the mirror to practice speech and enunciation. It came as no surprise to Mattie that she was crowned Miss Adams County 1951.

In the papers, radio programs and talk that circulated Adams County, Mattie was a major topic of conversation, right up there with Lana.

"Did you hear Mattie Doyle won Miss Adams County?"

"It's fate, I tell you. A girl that pretty was just meant to be Miss Adams County. I wonder what she'll do with the $250 she won."

"And did you hear about Lana Turner?"

"No, what?"

"They say her husband did some ungodly things to her daughter."

"No, really? Like what?"

"I can't repeat things that awful."

So circulated and diffused the lives of Mattie and Lana.

With her $250, Mattie packed her bags and set off for Hollywood. Mattie thought that being Miss Adams County would get her somewhere and it did — the Lincoln Motel on Sunset and Vine. Mattie found herself a night-shift waitressing job, leaving her days free to do auditions and cattle calls. In her spare time, Mattie would go to the Sunset Theatre down the boulevard from the motel and see Lana.

Mattie watched Lana in *The Bad and the Beautiful*, with Kirk Douglas as her leading man this time. On the veranda, Kirk rested his right arm on the railing, with a cigarette dangling from his left hand. Lana stood in front of him, longing to feel Kirk's strong hands squeeze her flesh between his fingers. But he stood with his eyes diverted, indifferent to her longings. Lana pleaded her love for him, her need for him; Kirk scoffed at her words and laughed.

Kirk dragged on his cigarette and exhaled in her direction. Lana closed her eyes, surrounded by his white, hot breath, swirling around her like a demon dog. Kirk removed himself from the railing and started to move from his place, but Lana stood in his way. He grabbed her, shook her till tears fell from her eyes, then left her there, alone on the veranda with the spillage of her warm tears.

Mattie watched the confrontation, afraid and ashamed for Lana. She listened to the quick thumps of her heart, and noticed her hands clutching the red angora sweater which clung to her body like sweat.

After the movie, Mattie wandered the Hollywood streets till she found herself outside Schwab's Drug Store, where some of the sign's neon letters had ceased working, so that it read "Schwa." Mattie was too excited to notice as she rushed in through the glass doors. She sat at the counter and ordered an iced tea. Mattie looked around the interior of the pharmacy, and noticed the chrome-accented stools. Lana's body had rested on one of these, she thought. Mattie could not think of a plausible way to rest her body on all the stools and occupy the same seat as Lana had, without appearing eccentric, or without coming to Schwab's everyday.

Mattie noticed an autographed picture of Lana at the far end of the counter as she sipped from her tea. She stared for a while making sure it was Lana, before she got down off her stool. A man passed over to Mattie as she started to make her way toward the picture and inquired, "Excuse me, Miss. I don't mean to sound insincere, but are you an actress?" Mattie didn't know how to respond, for though she'd come to Hollywood to become a movie star and had been to many auditions, she still hadn't landed a single part.

"My name is Paul Mayer," continued the gentleman. Mattie was immediately taken by this man dressed in a navy suit, who'd been sitting at a table near the door.

"Mayer," thought Mattie, the name echoing in her mind as a Hollywood name.

"Do you mind if I sit," asked the gentleman, pointing to the adjacent stool. Mattie's head shook, automatically.

"What's your name?"

"Mattie Lynne Doyle."

"Mattie Lynne Doyle, hmm? That's a nice name."

"Do you think so?"

"Sure, don't you?"

"No, not really. It's so plain and boring — there's no glamour."

"Oh, it's glamour you want? How about...'Desiree Doyle?'"

"That's horrible. I want a beautiful name like Lana Turner," said Mattie, pointing to the picture at the far end of the counter.

"I gave her that name, you know. Her real name was Julia Jean Turner."

"No! Did you really? I can't believe this! Are you the producer who discovered her?"

"I certainly am."

Their conversation carried on till late in the evening. The gentleman, through casual conversation, got to know all about Miss Adams County. He offered Mattie a ride home and she accepted. Ascending the stairs to her room, the man laid his hand softly on Mattie's lower back, sending cool vents of air up her spine. She offered him a cigarette and he accepted. He offered to make her a star if she had sex with him, and she accepted. In the dark room, they lay beneath a canopy of blue smoke colored by the neon lights of the Lincoln Motel.

While Mattie was still asleep, the gentleman left without a word, note, or business card. Mattie awoke and found her room filled with nothing but cold emptiness. She returned to Schwab's later in the day, hoping to find Mr. Paul Mayer, but he wasn't there. This time, she sat on the far side of the counter staring at Lana on the wall. The man behind the counter said, "Beautiful, ain't she?"

"Very," said Mattie, softly.

"Yeah and she's great for business, too."

"Really? How?"

"Well, you know that story about how some movie big shot found her sitting in here? It ain't exactly true. They just needed a gimmick to make her more famous."

Mattie remained in Hollywood a few more years, waitressing, but no longer auditioning. She journeyed home in the fall of 1958, back to her father's ranch. Mr. Doyle met her at the Billings bus depot and they commenced the twenty-seven mile drive. Mattie was arriving on the tails of the words that preceded her.

"Did you hear Mattie Doyle is coming back?"

"No, really? Why?"

"Don't know. I hear she just didn't make it in Hollywood."

"Poor thing."

"And did you hear about Lana Turner's boyfriend?"

"No, what happened?"

"Her daughter took a knife and stabbed the man to death! Can you believe that? They say he was involved in the mafia, but that's not why she killed him."

"Really? I wonder if Mattie would know anything, being in Hollywood and all."

On the roadside, Mattie's skeletons laid quietly under an

early cover of late fall snow. As she approached town, Mattie inducted a fresh carcass near the "New Hope 20" sign. But this one had no name.

Two Haiku

By Edwin Grey

scum covered black pond
lies hidden in Durand Park
minnow thwarts stillness

in morning sunrise
encumbered cherry branches
bow to misty ground

Swallow

By Jonathan Sherwood

I'm lying, head in her lap, belly full of pizza, quiet and drifting off to sleep. I'm not really sure what she's doing because I'm getting lost in that fog of slumber. Her fingertips glide gently and kindly over my features in such a way that it almost feels as if she's pulling a blanket over me, and content, I sink into the sensation. She trails her hand across my lips and I exhale against her palm. Perhaps it was the moisture of my breath on her skin, or I unsettled the aroma into my direction, but when I inhale, I smell her. I smell the metal of the doorknob. Toothpaste. Ink from a paperback. I smell the soap she washed with and the towel that dried her. Somewhere, she flipped through a magazine with a perfume ad. Leather. Scent of her hair when her fingers had combed through it. I am still motionless but no longer passive. Every cell in my body has taken attention, like tired workers passing unbelievable gossip to one another. The call to arms has gone out. Arteries widen, skin sets its hair erect in a wave like a caterpillar's back, jaw reels itself tight. Every piece of me has stood up, and turned to look at her. My untired eyes open. She notices and smiles lovingly at me, tracing my hairline with a kindly touch. My teeth grate. I'm going to swallow her.

Imprisoned by *Mary Wargo*, linoleum print, 1992.

St. Patrick's Day

By Patrick Callan

Hooray for St. Patrick who drove the snakes
(or something) out of Ireland forever!

Let us leave work an hour early
In honor of this, our favorite
Unholy holiday.

Tell our friends to meet us at McGinnity's at five
To catch the blessed buzz and
Stain our tongues and teeth green
With the welcome dose of delirium,
And arrogantly oblige
The cute Italian girl with the pin.

We'll break rocky Irish soda bread together,
Order another pitcher
And plates of the reeking corned beef and cabbage,
And call the taxi while we can still dial.

We'll fake and slur the words about the smilin' eyes,
Hook our arms hard around each other's neck
And cry about a country we'll never see,

Never want to see.

Erin go to hell
And God bless America!

Tragedy

By Patrick Callan

Chirping grey sparrows punctuate
the sunny morning chill of late October.

Fresh out of school,
I, the pressed and polished new English teacher,
ease into my brand-new car.

Crisp leaves crinkle under
the slow roll of gripping black rubber
as I back over the blacktop driveway with care.

The car dips slowly, heavily over the gutter,
and for a moment I feel watched
as I remember my father's words,
"Go slow or you'll squash somebody."

I round the corner
and brake —
two blinking roadside jalopies,
the doors left desperately ajar,
pointing to the motionless teenager
stretched out on her back on the freezing cement.

Her golden hair splayed like a halo
over the pavement around her head,
the C-trick Samaritan straight from work,
with grimy hands and worried eyes,
methodically rubs her shaking shoulders and limbs.
My balled coat makes a crude pillow
as I slide it gently beneath her heavy head.

The shrill sirens drown the wails
of the pacing, drunken woman who struck
this beautiful woman-child
on her fateful jog before school.

As paramedics remove her small sneakers,
poke the arches of her feet with a small orange pick,
she murmurs tearfully, "I can't feel my legs."
They slide a scraped blue board beneath her,
hoist her onto the huge gurney,
and sirens scream away
to the hospital and jail.

I take back my crumpled coat,
warm on one side.

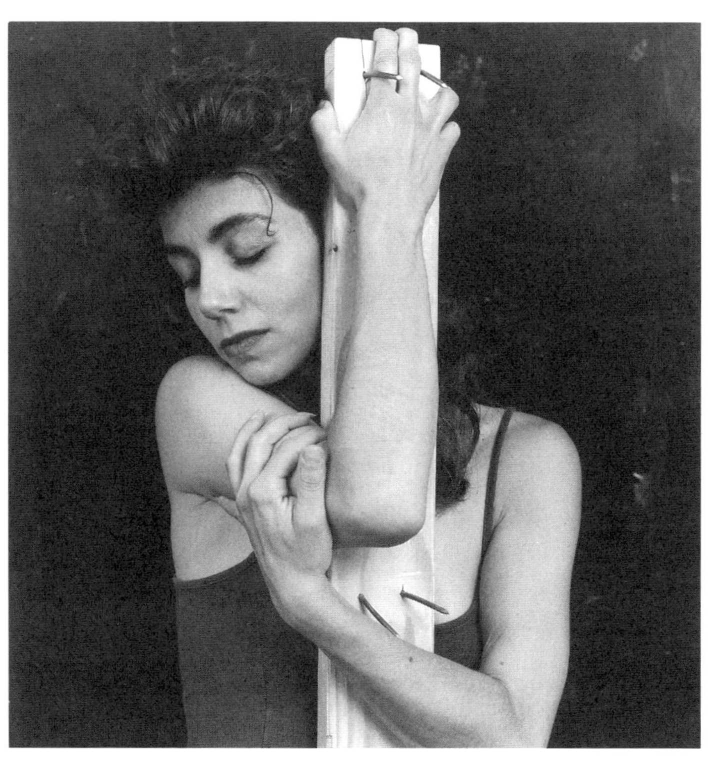

Woman with Board and Nails
by Roy Sowers

This Fall

By James E. Walker

CIRRUS CLOUDS ARE ALL I CAN SEE AS the ambulance races through the midday streets to a hospital I have never visited before. I am not going to die, I have convinced myself of that. The oxygen has filled me with a sense of calm. Compare that to a half hour ago when I was reeling about with my disconnected head and buzzed-out, shaking hands, trying to call either an ambulance or my mom, and I have come a long way. But for that bad fifteen minutes, I felt I was going to fall off the earth screaming through my unconsciousness for no one to hear. Quite frankly, it was my first brush with helplessness, mortality.

"Would you like something warm to hold onto?" Annie, the EMT, asks as she leans forward into my field of vision.

I look down at my hands which I was unknowingly rubbing together. I look to Annie's face. I see a heart in this woman's face and feel a caring that only comes from understanding. I have woken up the past two evenings in the middle of the night shivering, holding a pillow to my chest like some lost lover. Somehow she knows this.

"Yes, please." Can she hear me through this mask? I lift it and reply again, "Yes, please."

I watch her cross in front of my bed to a glass cabinet. Her full body exudes a strength that I am sure her job requires. She breaks the inner seal of a heating pack, smiles and hands it to me.

Sara, my most recent ex-girlfriend, hangs silently on the other end of the line. I am waiting.

I want you to be weak. Don't get tough on me now.

"You're the one who broke up with me. I'm the one who needs distance now and you don't understand that?" She pauses. "Stop playing with me. This just isn't fair."

This is no time for distance.

"I just need someone to talk to." This is as close to begging as I will come. However, I will plead later, in the dark, alone.

"No, John, even that is too much for me right now. I know you have not been feeling well and I am concerned about you. But I need to adjust and part of that is not talking to you or seeing you for a while. Do you understand that?"

I had never heard her so calm and confident. But it is only making me feel sorrier for myself and angrier at her.

"I understand. You need to look out for yourself. That only makes sense."

"I never thought I would feel guilty telling you we needed more distance between us."

"I know." My enemy, silence, breaks in to tell me that there is nothing left to say. "I'll talk to you...whenever." The self pity is taking over and she has sensed it but is not succumbing to it like she has in the past.

"Okay," she breathes.

From what I can see through the small window in the door, the ambulance is slowing under a bridge. We speed up and I see sky again. No clouds now, only blue expanse. Somehow the slow movement of sky through the window frame is helping me hold on. Staring out at the softest blue my eyes have seen since I broke up with Beth, I am no longer frantic to change my perspective for fear of falling. I am holding on, so much so that I am even beginning to doubt that I am truly ill. But I have decided not to say I am sorry.

Annie is talking to me. I turn to her face at risk of losing the fine equilibrium I have achieved.

"How are you feeling?" she asks as she pulls up my sleeve again. "I'm gonna check your blood pressure one more time before we get to the hospital. We're about ten minutes out."

Her voice has a sweet tone but I know she is going to do whatever she wants. But that is what I want from her, to take liberty of action within the confines of caring for me. I want to give myself up and feel warm in her care.

"I'm feeling better. My hands are still numb." I raise them from the heating pack, immediately feeling them embraced by the cool air. I look down to see if they are shaking. They are not, really.

"Usually the oxygen slows the dizziness and your blood pressure is getting back towards a more normal level." She's smiling as she tells me this news. It should be interpreted as good news but I am not entirely pleased. I will not apologize, to anyone. I look back out the window.

Then there was Susan. I am still writing to her, but I don't believe I have even come close to denting her newly-formed armor. They all get so damn mature after I leave them. Of that, she is definitely the queen. I thought I would have her forever. The things she let me do. I did not carry on with other girls. No, I simply ignored her to the point where I felt so lonely that I would go back to her. She cried for weeks when I finally broke up with her, and sat by the window for the whole campus to see what I had done. But I had left her not for other interests, rather out of boredom. I was convinced I had done the right thing. And so were my friends. Of course, they all assumed I had something else secreted away on the side. Nope. Just boredom, boys. I was sure I had killed her with my neglect. But now, when I wanted to resurrect her, I found she had crawled out alive and was going to kill me the same way I had almost killed her.

I look from my slow moving picture frame to Annie's face. She's writing something about me on a gray and white form. I see the word "decrease" and a series of numbers come out of her pen.

She looks happy. I am not a boring patient. By how much

she's writing, I don't think I am a false alarm. The care she's giving me is warranted by my condition.

"How's that heating pack, still warm?" she asks as she reaches out and touches the part that escapes between my hands. "Its a little cold. I'll get you a new one."

She crosses in front of me again. She must be at least twenty years my senior. That only endears her more to me. Her khaki vest swings open as she reaches into the glass cabinet. In her navy, pilled turtleneck rest two soft, round breasts. Her buttocks curve the same way her breasts do. Softly.

"Here you go," she says, handing me the fresh heating pack. The smile continues to radiate from her face. Now I am convinced I am not a bother. Possibly I am even getting special care from her. She cannot be this nice to everyone.

"Thank you."

"Alright Matty, have a good time. Say 'hello' to Teresa for me." I was trying to be sincere. I hardly know my best friend Matt's new girlfriend. But, since she now owns him, I figure I should be nice.

"I will. Hey, I'll talk to you on Wednesday."

"Alright, talk to you then. Bye."

The room is still. The ringing in my ears is all I can hear. The air inside my room moves only when I want it to. This is a stillness that only exists in the suburbs, after all the leaves have fallen, when it is too cold for the grade-schoolers to go outside and there is no snow to overcome their dislike for the chill.

Every year I am taken by this late fall depression that is only relieved by the romantic first covering of snow. It is then that I can revisit the memories of young, very young lovers brought together and the fear of the rolling tires crunching ice up the driveway.

But this fall, the gray of the leafless tree in our front yard hardens my loneliness. As the wind sways its top branches in front of my window, I am sure that that first snow is never going to come.

We are slowing down. I can feel the ambulance make a short, sharp turn and immediately start backing up.

"We'll have you inside the hospital in a matter of seconds. When we get inside you have to remember they are very busy so moan a little," Annie says as she puts the back of her hand to her forehead and gives a low, rumbling example.

"Honestly?"

"Honest." She smiles down at me.

I feel her attention and her desire to work us to the front of the line. It's like we are some kind of a team now.

Annie opens the back door and struggles with two other EMT's to get my stretcher out of the ambulance. Annie stays on my left as if she knows that is where I am accustomed to having her. *No sudden changes. This sick young boy cannot handle it at the moment.* The two other EMT's take positions to my right.

We glide inside through the automatic doors and into the emergency room. It is not quite the frenzied, maddening rush of scurrying MD's and bleeding, stumbling patients that I had always suspected. The pace is quick and fluid. I assume everyone has a place to be.

"Hi, Bob," Annie's nurturing voice greets an oncoming man. I assume he is another EMT by the way he is dressed.

"Hi, Annie. What are you bringing in today?" the man asks as he reverses direction and walks along with us.

"John here suffered acute dizziness and numbness in his arms. But he seems to have stabilized for now."

The man looks down to my face.

"Hi," I say as I look from his face to his name tag. Robert Green.

"How ya doing?" his tone is a little loud but he puts on that he cares.

"Better now, but my arms are still kind of— "

"Hey Bob, are you heading back towards the village?" Annie asks in a quicker tone than I am used to hearing her use.

"Yeah, right now as a matter of fact. Do you need a ride?"

"Please."

We have now stopped at the end of a line of what I think is about four beds. Above the first bed in line, hangs a sign, "Triage." Annie hands my file across my body to one of the other EMT's.

"You and Marcy will be taking the ambulance back, right?"

"Oh yeah, as soon as we get this patient a doctor," she says smirking with some sort of "we do this everyday" humor.

"You know where to reach me," Annie says as she starts to turn her body in the direction of the door and taps her beeper for effect.

I am horrified by what I am learning. She's leaving me. She's leaving me in someone else's care. My head begins to spin again as I try to concentrate on Annie's face. Can't she read from my eyes that I need her?

She steps back toward my bed and puts her hand on my shoulder. "You make sure they check you out good and figure out what is causing this, okay?" I can no longer concentrate.

I cannot believe she is leaving me. What about our team? What about her commitment to take care of me? Can't she see the need in my face?

She's already walking away. My head is spinning faster than it was before I called the ambulance. My hold on consciousness is slipping away and I am fighting the urge to be frantic.

"Oh, John." I can hear her walking back towards me. Possible salvation. I am still holding on. Her hand rests on my shoulder and I raise my head to look at her. The room is still moving but I can see her.

"Don't forget to moan a little," she smirks as she raises the back of her hand to her forehead and lets out another low moan. "Bye, John." She pats my shoulder and walks off behind me.

As the pressure in my head takes away my sight, I hear her laugh.

Clean

By Ellen Paulini

Yesterday I pulled a black-winged bird
out of my chest and taught her to fly.
Claws dragging on my insides,
screeching and squawking the whole trip,
I introduced her to the daylight in one terse yank.

But now I think that I was tricked.
For an instant I had forgotten how good her black wings felt
fluttering swiftly, softly stroking against me deep inside.
How her loud screech was, to me, like a purr in my ear.
The pleasure of her dark song churning
in my guts, my legs, my hands and the ends of my hair.

I am so clean now I don't know where to go.
There are no hearts in this house tonight.
Ideas come, visions as colorful and naked as any,
and I try to squeeze them out through a ball point.

8:00, Noon, & 7:30 Clockwork

By Marc McGee

Her breasts ((being of
considerable flesh)
no larger, though, in fact,
than on the day she first
passed my bird cage (fastidious
in my methods of nothing
(squelched in the smell of
day-old papers and chlorine))
walking that poor old basset
in the same direction every
day since, 3 x's/day (((the
same direction as the clock
flushes, as the toilet ticks, as
any rookie stock racer's head
after Daytona) the hound &
the block & the breasts
ever tireless in the
madness of the familiar)
each tree placed at the
precise point of optimum
peeing & colonization (no
gas, food, or lodging signs

posted for some oasis (the tree
outside my window being one) thirty
miles off) where she stops,
waits for the reacquaintance
(so prim in her patience) they
hang in proper respect for
1 dog's duties (1 dog's and
his best (bird cage) friend's
(pecking away at his cuttlebone))
& after such a climax
(she does as she could only do)
folds away quietly, zigzagging
across cement squares (rest stop
to oasis) holding the pole to
rover & any driver who by
pure circumstance (not luck
or chance) motors by all eyes,
(finally retiring to her shampoo
flavored box spring))) were large.

The Shopping Cart Races

by Marc McGee

The shopping cart races
((not so distant from ourselves)
periodically remind us
(eternal in the pursuit
of virgin park (teenage
alluring) bushes & trash
bins (welded disdiffidence
to alarms set, naps & (city
spread) sex (sponsored by
your local north side returnables
& beverage headquarters (several
jaunted quadrants by blocks
from where (while sitting with
myself) I feel the knuckle
numbing fingerless gloved grip
(ratta tat tat)))
shakes us awake (counting the
numberless aisles (never
ceases to stop (the (cross-eyed)
most steadfast of speedwalkers))
marking (rhythmically) the empty

(cradle-robbed) dumpsters
(hitting the (Reebok laced
(no doubt the Howard Hughes
of homeless)) clutch,
Mario Andretti (as we
sometimes call him ((being
(of course) the pinnacle
of speed icons past (not
iconoclasts)))) steering through
the debris of others))))
the way such things
(city refuse) in life (love &
(fingernail) obsessions) are)
eddy & ebb.

Woman in the Mist
by Lara Lomac

Reign of the Superman:

An Exploration of Laurie Anderson's "O Superman," After the Fact

by Michael Tomczyszyn

THE FIRST THING ONE NOTICES IS THE annoying, pulsing drone of the percussion track on this 8:21 opus — a sampled, breathy monosyllable of Anderson's voice repeated over and over without syncopation or variation. After a while, if one is attentive, one notices how completely this effect is far beyond our notice, much less our continued annoyance. Hazarding a guess from my intuitive grasp of the song, the idea is to simultaneously humanize and mechanize the essence of the music.

The central time-keeping device is the most elemental, the most fundamental, primal, instinctive musical instrument available to man — the human voice. At the same time, this pre-historic impulse is processed in an electronic and dehumanizing manner. This feeds directly into the focus of the lyrics, and is ultimately the impetus of all of Anderson's music. She questions, redefines and re-envisions what exactly it means to be human in the 20th Century — to be an organic, visceral, living thing plugged everyday into all-pervasive technological systems of transport, information, life support, communication, nutrition, etc. (The name of the album on which this song appears — her first — is *Big Science*, for goodness' sake).

Even our most basic and primeval drives and impulses are

intimately (irrevocably?) plugged into the great digital world village. For example, rock & roll — perhaps the most vital and direct expression of our unbridled Dionysian instincts — is helpless without 120 volt AC power outlets. It is every day drawn more and more into processes of digital sound production, processing and reproduction, as well as computerized distribution and sales systems. Without these, rock & roll could not exist, much less reach people on the scale that it does. More than at any other time in history, we are becoming cyborgs — walking intermeshings of the natural and the artificial combined as interactive, co-dependent systems. And the possible paths lying before us point toward this as a continuing trend.

At heart, Anderson seems fascinated by this process of gradual fusion of man and his machines. Her songs both portray and enact that evolution, sketching out the effects each side has on the other as they are drawn increasingly into each other. "O Superman" in particular seems an early revelation and explication of the attraction, as well as horror, of this hybridization. It reveals and explains how the human finds herself wishing to express something seemingly and completely independent of technology (or, in this case, *about* technology), realizes that she was wired into an all-surrounding system before she was even born. Enveloped by the machine while she slept, she realizes that she requires it to simply comply with her inborn need to reach out to another human being and share something poignant.

In "O Superman" the process of the song mirrors our own growth into outlets this information age gives us. To wit, we are lulled by the hypnotic seduction and beauty of the music as it bubbles rhythmically on, layered tastefully with synthetic strings. It is only in the last verse that we realize we can no longer tell for certain if it is the woman behind the machines who possesses and creates the aesthetic (the experience that drew us in to begin with), or if it is the machines, or the interaction of the two.

This perhaps even slaps us in the face further with the realization that *we* have been intimately pulled in. *We* have been linked up almost subliminally to this connection of human and machine, and the strangely fascinating, compelling art created by the fusion of ancient instincts with the freedom new technology gives us to express them. Too late to pull them out, we see the wires running under our own skin, linking digitized information processing with all of our grandiose notions about the elusive and enigmatic sanctity of human cognition.

It is with chilling empathy, then, that we hear the final lines of the song:

> *So hold me, Mom, in your long arms.*
> *In your automatic arms. Your electronic arms.*
> *In your arms.*
> *So hold me, Mom, in your long arms.*
> *Your petrochemical arms. Your military arms.*
> *In your electronic arms.*

It is fitting that these lines receive particularly dramatic musical backing. They are absolutely key to the deepest truth she has to share with us about the world which we may be (un)lucky enough to wake up to and understand in all its terrifying and brutal majesty.

She strikes an especially powerful note when she twists Orwell's "Big Brother" into a maternal figure. First, it punches all the ugliness of this realization deftly home by desecrating the most untouchable, warm, "human" figure we know in our lives. What could be more profoundly frightening than finding steel and circuitry relays under your mother's skin? What could put an icier hand on the back of your neck than realizing your umbilical cord is a fiber-optic line and that your familiar world is nothing more than a cathode womb?

Second, it establishes the absolute necessity at this late stage in our history of this relationship, its pure unavoidability. We are raised, nurtured, and guided by the "long arms" of this society of computer-assisted efficiency we have constructed, and by its guardians — the technocracy, the high circle of specialists with the authority and know-how to most effectively manage this construct.

This brings us to perhaps the most fear-inspiring of the revelations to be gleaned from Anderson's song. Though we are left with awful shivers at the thought of being swallowed up by a serpent with access to fax machines, cellular phones, and virtual reality technology, there is the horrible certainty that we cannot tread back along this path we have taken. It is therefore imperative that we learn more and understand the tools which place us at the disadvantage of ignorance in relation to this system. "You don't know me, but I know you," says the technocrat in the song, and thus the raison d'etre for Anderson's investigation and warnings. But what exactly is the alarm all about?

It is the realization that there exists the very real danger of losing everything which ever made us wild, free, irrational, lustful, compassionate beings with warm blood, guts and pained brains with unfulfillable desires burning in our hearts.

'Cause when love is gone, there's always justice.
And when justice is gone, there's always force.
And when force is gone, there's always Mom.

In three succinct lines Anderson powerfully kicks us with the painful awareness of the escalating levels of devolution and degradation the human soul is subject to when it too rashly pursues the alluring call of science. This horror is exemplified by the continued anti-perfection of the methods our rulers (I'm loathe to call them "leaders") devise, revise, and enforce to rule to their fullest ability. She doesn't go so far as to point at the technology itself as causative of this ominous evil (the caveat is coming from a woman who is herself thoroughly conversant with many aspects of modern technological innovations), but the point does seem to be that these wonders of science make the execution of all the abuses inherent in existing power structures that much more expedient and palatable. It makes them conscionable, in that our Jiminy Crickets are being systematically snuffed out and silenced by the thick blanket of convenience and comfort that this system provides. "This is the hand, the hand that takes," and what it takes most often is what makes us different from machines to begin with.

Again, it perhaps doesn't necessarily have to be quite like that, but this is one danger which clearly needs to be guarded against as we march closer and closer to the realization of our "brave new world."

Perhaps the most disturbing aspect of this is the unsettling mix of feelings one has toward this metamorphosis. While there is a strong mistrust and fear felt by anyone with even the tiniest shred of neo-Luddite caution, if one sits quietly and listens carefully for a long moment, there is an attraction underneath the trepidation. This state we are hurtling toward at breakneck speed is, after all, perhaps no more than the logical extension of everything the opposable thumb has meant in shaping our identity as human beings. There is perhaps really no way to avoid becoming inextricably bound up in the tools one uses — a thing is, after all, no more than what it does. From a step taken behind the vantage point one's temporal, provincial ideology gives one, there are perhaps no objectively verifiable lines to draw between the natural and the artificial, only arbitrary ones based on the prejudices of one's time and culture.

Maybe, then, the only choice lying before us is not that of *whether* to proceed, but *how* to proceed. There will of necessity be prices to pay for our gains — that is the inevitable nature of change. There exists no way to get from A to B while keeping everything one had at the start. The responsibility laid upon our shoulders now (and it is an absolutely crucial one) is to choose wisely and humanely what we are willing to give up for our progress, and what temptations we are willing to pass over in favor of maintaining the sanctity of our nature as thinking, feeling, wondrous creatures with hearts and souls, as well as minds.

So you better get ready. Ready to go.
You can come as you are , but pay as you go.

Portrait

By Maria Gillard

I've seen you before
greybearded man
gregarious catofsomekind
purring shifting dancing sneak
you sing me
sister teacher father cousin
roaring over kegs of beer
laughing loudly at children
hollering at the umpire

I've seen you on the marching field
bass drum behind the band
outfield ghost of willie mays shouting
pitcheminthereboy pitcheminthereno w

you grab the sports section first
choking down coffee
devouring corn and salt potatoes
biiiigg faaattt saandwiches

I HAVE seen you before
Irish Welsh spirit, Mr. Beard

unafraid and fearless
over and over
again and again

Mahogany Bedpost

By Maria Gillard

Mahogany bedpost

olive beige
bedspread

big cotton pillows
water lapping up the shore
beneath the window

balmy April wind

melting

TRUST

olive coils of skin
breasts
lips
velvet
purple
satin

tiny pearl

clutch

Stirring

By Maria Gillard

She stands at the stove stirring
She stirs and stirs
gravy
getting thicker and browner
with each turn of the spoon
Her spine straight, shoulders wide
legs strong and muscular
from years of chasing children, climbing stairs
Her black and brown cotton skirt hangs
to the backs of her knees
Her hair has been silver for years
though she is only 45

Piano music circles round and round on the Hi-Fi
plagued by the background sound of
pots clanging
glasses clinking
grease sizzling

Ivories tickling jazz
sing low blue lights
red candles

smoke and sweet vermouth
handsome men, azaleas
street lamps, Desotos

Melodies perk like coffee
and sweep through her kitchen
like a warm wind
perfumed with lilacs

She hums along as if SHE were the wind
in a hollow alley
stirring up the dust
the cobwebs
the night
to a rhythm all her own

Presidential Debates 1992

by Roy Sowers

Raging Berube

By Patrick Callan

"YOU *SUCK*, BERUBE!"

By then Dan could have taken it if it had come from anyone else. He could have heard it but just remained seated calmly on the bench with the second- and third-stringers. He might even have managed to counter by calmly raising a conspicuous middle finger in a faked nose rub. But not this time — not with this verbal assault shot over the shoulder of Dan's nemesis, Brandon Cowley, as he trotted across the infield to assume Dan's former position at second base.

Dan was a small, plain-looking boy of eleven. He had narrow shoulders and severely-combed, greasy brown hair parted on the side. He wore gold wire-rimmed glasses that further reduced his closely set, beady blue eyes. Cowley was twelve and an attractive, pretty boy with feathered blonde hair, a permanent tan and a toothy white smile — an intensely obnoxious boy with whom Dan competed fiercely for everything.

In her usual top-bleacher seat, Dan's mother cringed at these hateful, familiar words from the Cowley boy. Her heart sank as she instantly recalled the brouhaha at last week's game when Dan's uncommonly volatile temper exploded once again.

He had struck out his first at bat, and ignited by Cowley's consoling words, "You SUCK, Berube," hissed through the chain-link backstop behind him, Dan spun wildly and hurled his aluminum "Bombat" in blind rage in Cowley's direction. The bat crashed cacophonously against the fence, narrowly missing the squatting catcher and painfully nicking the left elbow of the umpire who, as it happened, was the commissioner of the little league that year. The angry, wounded commissioner instantly ejected Dan. Worse still, he sentenced Dan, still in full uniform, to go up and sit with his mother in the bleachers for the duration of the game at hand.

"You SUCK, Berube!" and Dan's mother knew that not only were these words injurious enough to provoke Dan, but that Cowley had now sinned cardinally against him: he'd added insult by appropriating that perverse, grating mispronunciation of Dan's French surname, properly pronounced "BAYruBAY," and blasphemed with the unforgivable "BerOOB."

Like a nightmarish film festival of embarrassment, this, in turn, suddenly triggered in her mind the stinging memory of when Dan was cut from the summer soccer team the previous year.

It had been an unfortunate oversight on the part of the busy coach. Dan's name had managed to elude the first, second, and then final cut lists. He had attended the congratulatory first team practice, was issued his maroon-and-white-striped team jersey, and even played some in the team's first scrimmage. It was only moments after the shrill sound of the referee's whistle marking the end of the first quarter that Dan, sweating and winded, was told gravely by a teammate to report to the team locker room and review the final cut list. He did so, and found his last name, radically misspelled, scrawled hastily in pen beneath the others. Fittingly, the whole outrageous blunder was made official with the sloppy signature of "Coach Garibaldi, " the Supremely Sensitive.

"Just ignore him, Danny," offered his mother, weakly. But she knew her son. She knew it was too late. Ripping off his cap, Dan sprang from his bench and tore across the finely-combed dirt infield after his enemy. Cowley giggled excitedly and tried to sidestep the advance, but Dan would not be eluded. He lunged at Cowley, tackling him about the waist and driving him hard down into the dirt. Amid the low billow of dust and dirt forming between the mound and second base, two forms could be seen engaged in a ferocious melee of flashing elbows, grunts and dishevelled jerseys.

Mrs. Berube looked down in horror on this latest spectacle starring her son and braced herself for the inevitable wave of nausea accompanying a mother's acute embarrassment.

But the pre-game scuffle was broken up almost immediately. The pitcher hustled over and pried himself between the two combatants, followed closely by the third baseman and shortstop who seized and separated them from behind. After a moment, Cowley began to laugh delightedly. Shaking himself loose from his restrainer, he found his hat, straightened his jersey and hissed again, "You SUCK, Berube!"

Dan was breathless and livid. By this time more players from the outfield and the bench had convened on the scene and encircled the boys to hide the unpleasantness from the parents, fans and now jeering opposing players. Dan's coach broke through the circle and assessed the situation as another one of "Berube's spasms." He grabbed Dan by the back of the neck and proceeded to escort him gruffly toward the bench, growling, between expletives, something about "embarrassment to the team" and "ass glued to the bench."

But they didn't stop at the team bench. As the other players returned to their positions and the game resumed, the coach marched Dan directly up to the bleachers. Without a word, he stuffed Dan down into the seat next to his mother. He gave her a look like you give the jerk at the beach who just cracked you in the head by accident with a frisbee, and stormed back down the planks, rejoining his team on the sideline.

The Berubes did not speak. They both just stared straight ahead — she in maternal mortification, and he with unbridled malice for Brandon Cowley.

As the innings passed, Dan looked on with silent, simmering contempt. Finally, in the bottom of the ninth with two outs and Dan's team down by a run, Cowley took the plate. He swung hard at the very first pitch and hit what looked like at least a stand-up double. Cowley rounded first, and as the ball dropped just in front of the hustling centerfielder, Cowley dug in and rounded second, heading for third. The centerfielder snatched up the ball on the one-hop and gunned it directly to third for the tag. Cowley ran furiously and then leaned back to slide in under the glove.

"SAFE!" barked the umpire.

But the ensuing burst of cheers for the apparent game M.V.P. was prematurely hushed. As some congratulatory teammates began to huddle around Cowley, they suddenly began signalling with urgent faces and flailing arms for the coach to come immediately. As the boys separated to admit the coach, Cowley could be seen writhing in the dirt, clutching his dirt-caked knee to his chest, his face twisted in a grimace of agony.

The sober silence pervading the field was eerie. It was punctuated by the coach's shout for ice and by Cowley's pathetic, choking sobs as he rocked to and fro, clutching his twisted knee.

For a few moments, no boy on either team spoke. No parent or child stirred in the bleachers. The people looked on compassionately with natural human concern for the injured lad, and quiet reverence for his sniffling mother as she made her way down the bleachers to console and support her son.

Dan could endure it no more. His cleats made a harsh, clattering noise on the bleacher as he sprang to his feet. In a loud voice, gesticulating with his arms in the air in a desperate, general appeal, cried, "It's his own fault! He doesn't know how to slide! HE DOESN'T KNOW HOW TO SLIDE!"

The incredulous and condemning heads of parents, players and the community in general turned and glared at Dan and his mother. They wondered, "What's wrong with the Berube boy? What kind of little monster could seize a moment like this to publicly criticize the sliding technique of his seriously-injured teammate?"

Mrs. Berube was mortified yet unsurprised, like the dog owner who has come to realize that despite her best efforts, she cannot prevent her excitable dog from spontaneously urinating on the legs of her guests.

Rejected and condemned, Dan fell silent and sank heavily onto his bleacher seat next to his mother. He stared miserably downward in indignation and disgust with society, a soothsayer misunderstood in his own time.

Together they slouched, mother and son. Shamed by association, Mrs. Berube hung her head tiredly next to her son's and shared the scorn. But in spite of his present adolescent lunacy, and with the incredible strength of a long-suffering mother's loyalty and love, Mrs. Berube believed in Dan. She just wondered how many more years her dream for her son's normalcy would be soundly deferred.

Lady in the Market

By Deborah Green

What the hell is
her problem
push in that cart
up and down the aisles
like she's got hours
to pick up just a few
things
look in so sad
like she's been hurt in
a long time
look in al most crazy
so people take to
gett in out of her
way
mov in like some
holy snail
sett in those TV
dinners and froz en
french style potatoes
down in that basket so gently
like they'd shatter in
to thousands of pieces
if she dropped em in

Alcohol Dreams

By Chris Moon

It's the laughter I remember most
Frisbee discs around the quad
And the smoke from the fire
Lifting over the hills
Drifting into the lilac sky

I remember
How we'd dance through the night
Under the strobe
Bounce off the walls
And lose control
How we ran through the graves
On the other side of the fence
Scared each other to death
Among the stones
How we'd shout at the vaulted sky
Shout as time slipped by
Until dawn rose and we fell
Company of rogues
All for one, one for all

Piled altogether
In our cinder block world
From our different past lives
We fell into each other's fearless arms
I know it wasn't long ago
I remember the faces
Some of the names
I still remember
I want to return
But there's no where to go
Without you all there again
To make it home
I want to return to—
Did I say how much...?
Alcohol dreams
And the music was so loud
Smoked fantasies
And we talked through the night
Sat under the Mother Sun
Heard the leaves in their whispering breeze
Closed our books and our eyes
And kissed the days away

Untitled by *Joshua R. Deaner*, silver gelatin print, 1995.

Lost and Found

By William Lung

"DO NOT LET HER FORGET! YOU MUST tell her, about you, about me and my mother before. Watch over her carefully, do not let her stray or you will lose her forever." That is what my mother said to me last night while I was in bed.

I saw her face outside my window, but it was not entirely familiar at first. She was young with dark, solid eyes, smooth white skin and bright, blood-red lipstick. I eventually recognized the face outside my window as the face in the antique wooden picture frame that adorned my mother's bureau, and now adorns mine. It was her wedding portrait from her marriage to my father taken some forty years earlier. She was so beautiful.

She drew her face further into the center of the window so that her body had space enough to be drawn into full view. Against the dark sky and amongst the branches of the white birch, she arose like a phoenix swathed in flames of red silk. The *cheong sam* she wore, I had seen dozens of times before. The dress had a hem of hand-crafted, white lotus blossoms that upon running into itself, started climbing up her left side, ending at her breast. In my mind, I remembered the dress from detailed descriptions of her escape from the invading Japanese, how she had attempted to transport anything of value, monetary and sentimental, with her. On my body, I remembered the gathered-up bunches of red silk on the basement floor that hid my feet — the dress for the little girl who was playing with her mother's grown-up clothes was too big.

My mother then slipped through the window, effortlessly like a large puff of colored smoke that hovered over my bed for a few seconds, then settled itself by sitting on the side of the bed next to me.

This was my mother's ghost.

I sat up and she cupped her cool white hands upon my feverish ones. She leaned closer. I watched her face closely and felt the squeeze of her hands on mine. She was beautiful, just like her picture. But, she had a troubled look that drew her eyes back, caused by years of disappointment and loss that distanced them from any deserved amount of happiness. I'm surprised I remember what she said. I was so dazed as she descended upon my bed. I stared at her, noticing the stark contrast of her bundle of jet-black hair that crowned her milken face and the red flames that fluttered like rose petals in the soft summer breeze. Slowly, I loosened my right hand from beneath hers and moved it closer to her face, wanting to trace my finger along her cheek to see if she were real.

Then a shrill cry tore through the room and in that instant, my mother disappeared. My hand remained at the point where it was about to touch her face and seconds passed before I could move again. I lunged forward, bringing the bedsheets and covers with me, trying to catch my mother. But all my hands could grab was empty, colorless air. Where my mother had sat on the bed was now only moonlight and shadows.

The cries persisted, but now they sounded farther away. For what seemed like an hour, I sat there. Eventually, my attention to the cries grew stronger. They again increased in volume, but were just gradually bridging my sense of loss with my sense of obligation.

I shook the last solid pieces of disbelief from my head, brought my arm across my legs and untangled myself from the web of sheets and blankets. I walked across the room with the cries sounding louder and clearer in my ears. I entered the nursery, bent over the crib and saw my daughter Daisy crying.

Jay thinks I'm crazy. I told him what happened when he got back from teaching one of his evening classes at Stanford. He tried not to laugh when he saw how serious I was. Jay said that I dreamt the whole thing, that it was "a subconscious discourse with myself, relating my newfound maternity to the estrangement from my own mother." I felt like shoving a psych book down his throat.

I wonder if my mother would have liked Jay. I met him at a publishing party a few months after she died. It was one of those overbearing functions where you're surrounded by empty chatter and leaving never happens soon enough. I had heard Jay boring a small crowd with his theory on "how Dickensian ideology has an immediate relevance to the maintenance of the modern political structure in Great Britain." So when he approached me as I stood between the crudites and the halogen lamp, I cringed in my standard black, spaghetti-strapped cocktail dress. It wasn't as painful as I had feared; he soon calmed my apprehensions by informing me that he reserved those sort of topics for people who only watch PBS. He then escorted me out to the balcony where we escaped the weighty conversation, and mourned the death of disco beneath the stars.

Now we've been together for three years, married for one with a beautiful four-month-old daughter. Jay's not Chinese, he's Jewish, but I think mother would've grown to like him anyway. I was thirty, single and childless — perhaps no greater shame could I have brought to my mother. But now I have someone to love, take care of me and father my children, and who eats just about anything, a trait my mother loved.

My mother never openly expressed to me how much she wanted grandchildren, though she would nag me with questions, like when was I going to settle down and how was my love life? That was her subtle way of letting me know. It is more or less expected that a woman of Chinese descent, approaching the age of twenty-five, should honor her parents with at least one grandchild. The guilt I feel about this alone gets to me sometimes, while other times it just snowballs with my guilt over having been an academic and occupational failure, too. But these are the guilts everyone feels. It is inherent in being anybody's child.

Jay thought it best I had some time to myself, so today he's home with Daisy. Food shopping for Chinese New Year is my plan for the day. I've been preparing for our big New Year's dinner. I invited all my relatives. My mother would be proud, I think. It's been frustrating trying to cook like her, to manipulate the cleaver with the ease that she had. It was as if she were an enchantress twirling silver stars in her hand, or a samurai warrior. But samurai are Japanese, and my mother would turn in her grave if she knew I compared her to those "*say yupoon*," those "damned Japanese." And of course she would follow that with, "they learned everything from us anyway."

Trying to imitate the cut of the black mushrooms for Mom's steamed chicken with ginger and Chinese sausage has been a resulting disappointment, too. Cutting them differently wouldn't make them taste different; they would still taste like black mushrooms. But now that I've tasted one, they have lost a bit of their black mushroom flavor. How could that be? It must be a loss of a deeper kind.

My shopping excursion takes me into the heart of Chinatown. I walk past the shops which cater to residents and tourists alike. The crowds walk about and I step off the steady-moving line of people to join a small group surrounding the bins of produce at a market that is spilling out onto the street. I sift through one of two bins of snow peas, looking for firm, bright green ones amongst the paler, yellow ones. Then it comes back to me.

We were food shopping in the late afternoon, after my mother had picked me up from school. She was towering over the bins of fruit and vegetables and me too, in my orange dress that stopped right above my knees and a yellow ribbon knotted in a bow on top of my head. She was picking string beans to make one of my favorite dishes that night, cooked with thin strips of beef, black bean sauce and lots of garlic. It seemed as if my mother were snapping every single string bean to see if it were tender enough. I was getting restless. I watched the people passing by, the more familiar people who looked like me, and the *bok gwu*, the "white ghosts" who didn't.

My eyes fell upon a store across the street, but more exactly, a doll in the store window. She had long, blond curls, a frilly pink dress and wide, round eyes. I wanted to get a closer look and I knew if I asked my mother, she would say I was wasting my time. I figured she would be picking the string beans for a while longer, and what harm could there be for an eight-year-old girl to cross the street alone? Slowly, I ventured away from my mother's side. I was standing between two parked cars, the one to my left still warm to the touch. I looked both ways, saw nothing, and took a few steps into the middle of the street.

Standing there in the middle of the street, I heard the low mumble of an engine and the rumble of tires and car parts hitting uneven, bumpy asphalt. I looked up, and coming from up the street was a white van. I stood there thinking how stupid I was to have left my mother's side, but didn't think of moving out of the way. The van was barreling towards me. My mother suddenly noticed I was missing, and scanned the street quickly. Spotting me, she shouted at the top of her lungs, "Siu-Mei! Siu-Mei! *Fihde juw!*" "Run quickly." Were it not for this, I probably would've been flattened like fortune cookie dough. The shrill sound of her scream weakened the hold the street, people, doll and white van had over me, and I regained my senses in time to run to the other side of the street.

My next fear was whether my mother was going to yell and beat me in front of a streetful of strangers, or wait till later so she could do it in the privacy of our home. She ran across the street, slapped me across the face and grabbed a hold of my arms, shaking me. Maybe she thought I was momentarily possessed by some evil spirit that needed to be expelled from my body with sharp jerks. She screamed, *"Nay hiy miy chse sen? Nay jo mutje?"* "Are you crazy? What are you doing?"

Then she did it. She hit me and yelled at me in front of a streetful of strangers. I began to cry, the tears streaming down my face. I felt this ball of red shame rising up from my stomach into my head, which I thought was going to explode. *"Deem guy?"* she asked me. "Why?" I couldn't answer her. I could hardly breathe. I just shrugged my shoulders and shook my head, unable to stop my body from hyperventilating, from convulsing. She threw her arms around me and smothered my face in her shoulder. After a while, I stopped crying and I could breathe again. Then she pulled me away from her body and asked me again, *"Deem guy?"* This time, after the struggle to complete my words, I answered her. "I wanted to see the doll,"

I said softly, pointing to the vision in pink that had caught my attention. My mother cast her eyes up to the doll, then lowered them, looking at the ground as if in defeat. She raised them again to meet mine and said, "I will buy you the doll if you promise never to go away from me. *Daying ngaw?*" she asked. "Promise me?"

I absently drop my bag of snow peas into the bin and start running towards my car. The drive home seems endless, though I am caught in my own world. I see my mother's face, now old, scrunched up and disapproving, staring at me from the rearview mirror. And I begin to hear echoes of her voice, superseding the car horns backed up behind me telling me the light has turned green. "Women drivers!" I hear someone shout. "Chinese drivers!" chimes in another. I finally get on the expressway where traffic is flowing, and I hear my mother's voice as the yellow lines disappear quickly beneath my car.

"When I was a young girl," I listen to the voice say, "I always got so excited at New Year's. The house would be so busy — servants cooking and cleaning, my mother and grandmothers supervising everything, everyone running around. I would sit in the courtyard and watch the kitchen girl kill fresh chickens. Then she would pluck their feathers and I'd watch them float about the girl and think it looked like snow.

"One New Year, when I was five years old, my mother shooed me from the courtyard and told me to have one of the servant girls dress me in my New Year's clothes. I was delighting in the falling feathers and would not leave. My mother then bargained that if I got changed, she would let me see the firecrackers that night. I had never seen the firecrackers before, only heard them. I was so excited that I ran through the dark hallways of the house, screaming that I could finally see the firecrackers. The servant girl who dressed me was excited for me too. As she pulled the new red blouse over my head, brushing and pulling my hair into a ponytail, she told me the firecrackers were in a link and that when they exploded it was like a chain of bright white flowers bursting in the air. The image of luminous, floating flowers engaged me so.

"After the big dinner, we all walked to the village square. The adults had been drinking and were talking loudly. The noise was overwhelming — laughter, chatter, drums for the lion dance, applause. My mother lifted me in her arms to see everything — all the people, the decorations, the dance. She tired of carrying me and no servant girls were in sight, so she set me down and told me to stay close. I held on to her pants as I watched a parade of people pass by. Then it was time for the firecrackers. The men laid a long chain of them in the street — there must've been thousands of firecrackers. Imagine that — thousands of pretty, floating white flowers. The chain started farther up from where we were standing, and I saw the pretty, bursting flowers and all the smoke. I wanted to have one of these flowers, so I walked up to the chain and tried to break one off. No one noticed, their eyes were all too busy following the thousands of mini-explosions down the chain.

"I had heard the pops getting closer, but was so persistent in trying to get a souvenir that before I knew it, I was surrounded by bursting white flowers and smoke and people trying to reach for me. All I could hear was 'POP! POP! POP! POP! POP!' a million times over, and I couldn't even hear my own screams.

"The doctor told my parents that I was fortunate enough to have been grabbed in time before any more serious damage was done. As it stood, I was mostly deaf in my left ear with some second- and third-degree burns that would scar. My mother didn't know whether to stand on my right side and yell at me so I could hear, or just console her little girl. She held me close, my left ear resting on her shoulder. I could hear her cry."

My mother's voice fades as the police siren sounds closer and the red light circles in the air. How am I going to explain this one? I pull over and the cop, not finding anything illegal, advises me to be a little more careful from now on. I proceed home, heeding the officer's advice. Nearing the house, I begin to panic. Frantically, I pull my car into the driveway and run into the house, hurrying past Jay and his bewildered look. I slip quietly into the nursery and Daisy is sleeping there in her crib, still safe, still full of promise. Daisy. That is her name, more or less. That is what I came up with. Daisy, or Daying-Sen, "promise fulfilled."

Contributors

Jayne Aquilina, a writer since age nine, has a B.A. in creative writing and an M.A.T. in teaching high school English. She has worked in two area bookstores — Village Green and Borders — and is now a copy editor/proofreader for a local advertising agency. Aquilina is also the poetry editor for *Rochester Shorts* magazine.

Christie Becker received her B.F.A. in painting and graphic design from The Savannah College of Art and Design. After graduation she worked in Los Angeles for Gemini G.E.L. making limited edition prints of works by Roy Lichtenstein. Becker currently works at the B Dalton in Irondequoit and is pursuing a Master's in art therapy at Nazareth College.

Todd Beers is the Poet-In-Residence at Writers & Books. Todd directed the innovative Strong Writers' Program at Strong Memorial Hospital, where he explored poetry with critically-ill children (*Waiting Room*, W&B Publications). A chapbook of his works *O* (pronounced "zero") was published by i Publications in 1995. *Poetry Motel* and *Permafrost* will include selections of his work in upcoming editions.

Gabe Billings spent two years as an undergraduate at RIT pursuing a photography degree, left to take some time off and soon found himself working at Borders Books & Music. He currently works there as a trainer, and in his spare time bakes cheesecake, wrestles goats at Lollypop Farm and beats Col. Richard LaPointe at pool.

Joshua Deaner was born in Boston. Currently he is a second-year student of photography at RIT. He works at Borders.

Maria Gillard is a singer/songwriter/musician living in Rochester. She has published two recordings of original music and performs in clubs and coffee houses throughout the Northeast. She is an employee of Borders.

Deborah Green moved to Rochester from California late last year. She taught English for several years in Los Angeles before entering the Peace Corps where she served as a secondary school teacher in Kenya's semi-arid Samburu land. She finds "ordinary" people to be the most extraordinary and fascinating of all. She works at the Village Green in Rochester.

Edwin Grey is retired and lives with his wife, Sharon, in Henrietta. He has been writing for fourteen years and has poetry placed in several publications. He worked a few days a week, as a non-paid volunteer, at Strawberry Hill Books in Pittsford, just to help out a personal friend.

Jessica Hill recently graduated from SUNY Brockport where she studied creative writing and photography. By her own admission, Hill's work is influenced by her family and her childhood on her grandparents' farm in western New York. She is currently working on a collection of prose and poetry that explores the early part of her life. Hill will publish a prose piece in the forthcoming *Where The Heart Is*, an anthology devoted to love and family.

Lara Lomac graduated from RIT with a B.S. in biomedical photography in 1993. After graduation, she volunteered to work on tree planting in Mozambique with The Institute for International Cooperation and Development (IICD). For a time, she worked at the Village Green in Rochester and has recently returned to IICD to volunteer in the promotions department.

William Lung graduated from the University of Rochester in 1994. After working at the Village Green in Rochester he recently moved back to New York City to pursue a career in the entertainment industry. *Lost and Found* is his first story and *An Imitation of Life* is his third and most recent.

Chris Moon, after two years of stumbling through the college routine, decided to formally study all those books he'd been reading anyway. He graduated from the University of Rochester in 1993 with degrees in English and Spanish. After college, Chris worked at Borders for two years and now lives in Seattle where he records his writings in 12-point Palatino and his music on 8-track dbx tape.

Ellen Paulini's only previous recognition for her writing was in the fifth grade when she won her school's nutrition writing contest. Although she has written for herself for years, "Clean" is her first published piece. She recently moved to Seattle and plans to continue writing both poetry and fiction.

Jonathan Sherwood, a Rochester native, worked for nearly three years at the Village Green in Rochester and more recently at Borders. Currently he is an editor for *Scene* magazine and a radio personality on 106.7 WMAX's morning show. "Swallow" is his first piece of published fiction.

Roy Sowers is an employee of Borders Books & Music.

Michael Tomczyszyn has lived in the Rochester area all his life, working a strange assortment of jobs along the way. He currently devotes much of his time to playing out and co-writing noisy pop songs with a local punk band, the Shoe-Gazers, and plans to become a Texan someday. Michael is a former employee of the Village Green in Greece.

Mary Wargo graduated from Nazareth College with a B.S. in studio art. She worked briefly with a local advertising agency before she realized that advertising was not for her. While working at Lauriat's Bookstore in Irondequoit, she is writing and illustrating a couple of children's books which she eventually hopes to get published.

Editors

Patrick Callan graduated from SUNY Geneseo with a B.A. in English with secondary ed. certification and has taught high school English. He also writes and has published short fiction and poetry in *Rochester Shorts*. An active member of Corpus Christi Church, Callan lives and works in Rochester and is earning an M.A. in English at SUNY Buffalo.

Abram G. Johnson was born and raised in Rochester, NY and is the only child of a college English professor (father) and a graphic artist (mother). Johnson received his B.A. from SUNY Oneonta in anthropology, with minors in geography and religious studies, and is now in graduate school at SUNY Buffalo. He works at Borders Books & Music in Rochester where he met his partners in publishing. Johnson is currently writing his Master's thesis in cultural anthropology on Mormon families. In his spare time he edits with his friends for Tinnitus Publishing, gets to wear various children's book character costumes at work for story-time and collects radioactive Vaseline glass.

Marc McGee, recovering from a bout with *weltschmerz*, lives in Boston and is enrolled in Emerson College where he is taking graduate classes in writing and publishing.

James E. Walker was born and raised in Maine. After receiving his B.A. in Latin American history from Connecticut College in 1993, he moved to Fairport, NY. He worked one year for Borders and spent the summer of 1994 studying in Mexico. Currently he is the Book Department Supervisor at the Village Green in Fairport.